陝西民間美術
Shaanxi Folk Arts

陝西民間美術

# Shaanxi Folk Arts

編　選：戴剛毅　郭佑民
攝　影：郭佑民
文　字：戴剛毅
設　計：王春霖

出　版：新民主出版社
　　　　香港九龍紅磡馬頭圍道39號
　　　　紅磡商業中心A座1015室

總發行：中國圖書進出口總公司
　　　　中國北京朝內大街137號

印　刷：輝煌印刷廠
　　　　香港鰂魚涌華蘭路18號
　　　　萬邦工業大廈18樓A座

一九八八年六月
第一版第一次印刷
ISBN 962•336•005•3

Complied by Dai Gangyi, Guo Youmin.
Photograph by Guo Youmin
Written by Dai Gangyi
Designed by Wong Chun-lam

Published by
Sinminchu Publishing Co.
Rm 1015, Tower A, Hunghom Commercial Centre,
39 Ma Tau Wai Road, Hunghom, Kowloon, Hong Kong.

Distributed by
China National Publications Import and Export Corporation
137 Chaoyangmennei Dajie, Beijing, China.

Printed by
Fairmount Printing Factory Ltd.
Block A, 18th Floor, Melbourne Industrial Building,
18 Westlands Road, Quarry Bay, Hong Kong.

First Edition June 1988
ISBN 962·336·005·3

# 陝西民間美術

## SHAANXI FOLK ARTS

戴剛毅　郭佑民選編　Compiled by Dai Gangyi and Guo Youmin
新民主出版社出版　Published by Sinminchu Publishing Co.

# 序言

中國有着極爲豐富的文化藝術遺產，民間美術是其中重要組成部分。它是"生產者的藝術"（魯迅語），是勞動人民的美的創造。在中華民族生長、發展的幾千年漫長歲月裏，正是勞動者自身所創造的民間藝術形影不離地伴隨着他們的生活，鼓舞着他們的鬥爭，慰藉着他們的心靈。它那豐富的品類，眞摯的鄉土內涵，濃郁的生活氣息，鮮明的地方色彩，以及創作中的浪漫主義藝術手法，受到國內外專家學者的讚賞和推崇。

這本畫册，薈萃了具有古老文化傳統歷史的中國黃河中游陝西地區的民間美術，它猶如簇簇爛漫山花，也是當地民俗風情藝術畫廊的展現。

在華夏大地上，黃河中游是中華民族文化的搖籃，早在原始時代，就有人類在這裏生息繁衍。陝西在歷史上相當長的時期內，曾是全國的政治中心和文化藝術最發達的地區。西安曾爲西周、秦、西漢、隋、唐等十一個王朝的都城，歷時一千一百二十餘年，是著名"絲綢之路"的起點，很早就和日本、朝鮮、印度、印支半島、中亞、西亞以至歐洲一些國家和地區有着經濟文化交流，通過絲綢之路，成爲東方文化的中心。已發掘出的質樸優美的半坡彩陶、唐俑，雄渾豐富的周代靑銅器、秦磚漢瓦、漢畫象石和聞名遐邇的陶塑"秦兵馬俑"，漢唐石刻、壁畫等，這些在美術史上具有典範性的作品，無不凝聚着古代民間匠師的智慧和才能。西安被譽爲"天然歷史博物館"創造了輝煌燦爛的古代文化，爲世界文明的發展作出了宏偉的貢獻。深入考察陝西的民間美術決不可忽視和割斷它的歷史淵源。

民間美術是服從於人的本性的需要而產生的。質樸勤勞的人民對生活的熱愛和眷戀之情在民間美術中有着鮮明的表露。它多不見經傳，正因爲它處於下層，植根於鄉土中，盛開在勞動羣衆的心田裏，它那獨特的藝術個性往往能喚起人們縷縷鄉情、鄉思和民族情感，也可以說它是升華爲藝術美的鄉情。

陝西的民間美術源遠流長，千百年來，它已形成了一套完整的審美體系，被歷代勞動者承襲而積累下來。其自然性和自發性，是其發生和發展的主要特徵。它認識生活和表現生活的方式，以有機的整體性、節奏和旋律感見長，善於憑直覺、印象、記憶和對生活的體驗、理解去綜合把握對象，使藝術形象大大區別於自然原型。它在氣質上直率、自然，不拘泥、不做作，生動、親切，所蘊含的思想內容曲折地寄寓形象的具體性之中，它寓理于情、寓情於形，樸中見巧，粗中有細，拙重幽默，同時喜於運用裝飾化的形象語言，注意運用寓意和象徵手法。陝西民間美術從古到今，都在不斷探求自強的民族之魂和民族素質，表現了炎黃子孫的開拓精神。

民間的美術燦若羣星，包括在衣、食、住、行、用各個方面。爲廣大羣衆所喜聞樂見。民間藝術家充分利用大自然給予的極爲普通的天然材料，就地取材，因材施藝，他們懂得並熟悉羣衆的審美習慣，對生活的感受是以羣衆的審美體驗爲前提的。他們的作品，以心造形，以理造形，以美造形，有的看起來似乎加工不多，但却匠心獨運，質樸純眞，包含着深刻的藝術哲理，不僅給人以美的欣賞、娛樂作用，而且也有認識和教育作用。情感是審美心靈的原動力，是審美創造的原動力，他們還在童年少女之時，就受民間藝術的熏陶，在從母輩習藝時，就在心靈中種下美的種子，落後的生產方式，封閉的經濟文化，擋不住他們想像的翅膀，在自己的藝術天地裏馳騁翱翔，他們愛美之心是永恆的。

加強民間美術的研究，無論從繁榮美術創作，繼承和發展民族民間藝術傳統，或從開展美術史、美學和民俗學等方面的研究工作、普及審美教育來說，都有重要價值。民間美術中數量最大的民間工藝所具有的實用和審美的雙重性，使得它把人民的物質生活和精神融滙在一起。從本畫册可窺見到陝西民間美術中所蘊藏的極其豐富的思想材料，它積累了勞動者按照美的規律把握世界的經驗、技巧和法則。它作爲一個歷史的見証和往事的信物，會隨時將蘊藏在它身內的鄉土風情散發出來，使人神往，使人沉醉。

民間美術是心靈的造物，它不是凝固的東西，它在滿足廣大農民的審美需要中穩定地發展着。作爲中國傳統藝術之一的民間美術，是社會審美心態和藝術家的審美心態的交織，又通過可感媒介的外化。它也將隨着時代的步伐而發展，同時代社會和人民生活同步前進。

戴向紅

一九八六年十月於西安

4

# INTRODUCTION

Chinese folk art is an important part of the country's extremely rich cultural and art heritage.

Folk art, in Lu Xun's words, is the "art of the producers"; it is the aesthetic creation of the labouring people. In the past several thousand years of the Chinese nation's growth and development, it is folk art that has kept company with the working people in their lives, encouraged them in their struggles, and given them comfort and consolation. Chinese folk art has won recognition and praise from experts both at home and abroad for its great variety, sincere rural content, rich flavour of life, distinctive local style, and its artistic approaches of romantism.

This album is a collection of the outstanding examples of the works of folk art of Shaanxi Province which, lying in the middle reaches of the Huang River (Yellow River), is rich in history and cultural traditions. It is not only a folk art gallery, but also a representation of local customs.

The middle reaches of Yellow River are the cradle of Chinese culture. The ancestors of the Chinese people have lived and multiplied the earth here since the primitive age. In Chinese history, Shaanxi had for a very long time been the political centre of the country and boasted the nation's most developed culture and art. Xi'an was the capital of the Western Zhou, Qin, Western Han, Sui, Tang and six other dynasties, covering a period of more than 1,120 years. The famous Silk Road started and ran westward from the city, which has long had economic and cultural contacts with Japan and Korea and, through the Silk Road, with India, Indo-China, Middle Asia, West Asia and some European countries and regions. It was once the cultural centre of the East.

Ancient artifacts found in the province include the unsophisticated, beautiful Banpo painted pottery and Tang figurines; the majestic and firm bronzeware of the Zhou dynasty; the bricks of the Qin dynasty; the tiles of the Han dynasty; the stone tablets bearing engraved images of the Han dynasty; the terra-cotta soldiers and horses of the Qin dynasty; and the stone cavings and murals of the Han and Tang dynasties. All of them are classic examples of Chinese arts, crystallizing in them the wisdom and skill of the artisans of the past. Xi'an, a city which is reputed to be a large history museum itself, has created a splendid ancient culture, and made a great contribution to the civilization of the world. When we take a close look at the folk art of Shaanxi, we must not overlook or cut it off from its historical origins.

Folk art is born out of human need. The unsophisticatd and industrious working people boldly embody their love of life in folk art works. Folk art does not find record in many Chinese classics because it exists among the lower classes, has its root deep down in the country and flourishes in the minds of the labouring prople. But its unique artistic style can often evoke one's past memories of his/her nativc place, nostalgia and national feelings.

Shaanxi's folk arts are of long standing and well established. In the thousands of years of their development, they have evolved a complete set of aesthetic standards, which the labouring people have accepted and handed down from generation to generation. The principal characteristics of their growth and development are naturalness and spontaneity. The folk artist is at his best in understanding and depicting life in its wholeness, and apt to show its rhythms and melodies. He relies on his intuition, Impressions and memories, as well as his experience and understanding of life to grasp the essence of the phenomena or objects he depicts, thus making the artistic images quite different from their original models. In artistic representation and expression, works of folk art are straightforward, natural, flexible, free from affectedness, vivid and intimate. They reside, in roundabout ways, ideas in particular images, reason in emotion, and feelings in concrete forms. Ingenuity is found in simplicity, exquisiteness in crudeness, and humour in clumsiness. folk artists also use decorative, figurative, allegoric and symbolic methods with magical deftness. Since ancient times, Shaanxi folk art has been seeking to understand and present the lofty spirit of the Chinese nation. It has given expression to the indomitable morale and character of the Chinese people shown in their constant efforts to open up new paths for devlopment.

Like a galaxy of brilliant gems, folk art embraces all aspects of daily life and is loved by the masses. The materials that most commonly used are the ordinary natural substances that come readily to hand. Folk artists are familiar with the aesthetic habits of the people, and their feel of life is based on the aesthetic experiences of the masses. In creating art forms, they are guided by their mind, reason and aesthetic rules. Some of their works seem to be crudely made, but they show great ingenuity, originality, simplicity and purity, which implies a profound philosophy of art. Works of folk art afford people not only aesthetic enjoyment and amusement, but also knowledge and education.

Love is the motive force of aesthetic appreciation, and the motive force of creation of the beautiful. Folk artists have been under the edifying influence of folk art since their early childhood, and a seed of beauty was planted in their hearts when they became apprentices to elder folk artists. Neither the backward mode of production, nor the closed economy and culture could keep them from spreading their wings of imagination and flying freely in their world of art. Their love for the beautiful is eternal.

It is important to promote the study of folk art, for the study will help promote the production of works of art; carry forward the tradition of national and folk art; conduct study of art history, aesthetics and folklore; and popularize education aesthetics.

Crafts, the largest category of folk art, perfectly combines the material and spiritual life of the people because they have both utilitarian and aesthetic value. From this album one can get a glimpse of the extremely rich ideas contained in Shaanxi's popular arts, which are a treasure house of the labouring people's experiences, skills and rules in representing the world in accordance with aesthetic laws. As a witness of history and a token of the past, folk art will always fascinate and intoxicate people with its local charm and flavour.

Folk art is born of heart. It is not something that has become rigidly fixed; instead, it steadily develops as it tries to meet the peasants' need for appreciation of the beautiful. As a form of the traditional Chinese art, folk art is an intermixture of the aesthetic psychology of society and the aesthetic psychology of the artist, which externalizes itself through palpable media. It will develop with history, society and people's life.

DAI GANGYI
October 1986, Xi'an

# 目次
# Contents

# 原始彩陶
## PRIMITIVE PAINTED POTTERY

彩陶是我國最早以彩繪紋樣與造型相結合的民間藝術，這些具有歷史文物價值和藝術價值的珍貴作品，是進入新石器時代的標誌之一，它是隨着農業的出現，定居生活的需要而產生的。它交織着當時人類對生活、對自然事物的概念。那言簡意賅的藝術效果，反映出我國先民善於對複雜事物作哲理概括，用單純明確的藝術語言來表現事物的特徵及其與周圍事物的關係，並濃縮凝凍成標誌性很強的紋樣，十分得體地顯示出族文化的風采。

西安半坡彩陶，具有很高的藝術成就。它是在陶器入窰以前就畫上去的，燒成後色彩附在陶器的表面，不易脫落，其器物紋飾除去一些由編織紋演繹而成的幾何花紋外，是由以魚紋爲主的水族動物紋樣而具有特色的。在一定程度上反映了當時人們的漁獵、採集和農耕的生活。這古撲的圖案形體，刻寫着那一代拙樸的文明，體現了多樣統一這一美的規律，映現着那個時代的現實和憧憬。

魚紋貫串於半坡類型文化彩陶的始終，魚的單獨紋樣表現出由寫實到寫意的系列的發展過程。後期的魚紋多用減形手法，只用魚的帶有特徵的某一部分，如頭、身子、尾來示意性的表現魚。魚紋和人面紋、鳥紋相複合的紋樣，形象地表現了五、六千年前先民們的生產活動和審美情趣。寄托了多麼聰慧的想像呵！

Painted pottery was the earliest form of Chinese folk art that incorporated coloured designs into objects. These are works of important historical and artistic significance because they are one of the signs marking the entry of human civilization into the Neolithic Age.

Painted pottery appeared with agriculture to meet everyday requirements when men no longer lived nomadic lives. It was an embodiment of early men's notions about life and nature. Its primitive simplicity is meaningful and has great artistic effect,demonstrating the ability of the ancestors of the Chinese people to generalize complicated things philosophically and use simple, explicit artis-tic language to bring out the basic features of objects and their relations to others. The highly symbolic decorative patterns correctly showed the elegance of clan culture.

Xi'an's Banpo painted pottery represents a high level of artistic achievement. It is first painted and then fired, with the result that the colour will not peel off. Most of the pottery objects are typically decorated with fish or some other aquatic animal motifs and occasionaly associated with geometric patterns which evolved from woven designs. The prevalence of animal themes reflects, to a certain extent, the importance of fish and other animals in the life of the people of that period —— a life of fishing, hunting, gathering wild plants and fruits, and farming. Their simple forms and designs give themselves a pristine look, representing the civilization of that period, embodying the aesthetic law of unity of multiformity, and reflecting the reality and ideals of that era.

The fish motif appeared on all the painted pottery objects of that period of the Banpo-type cultures, and the individual fish patterns showed a gradual change from realistic depiction to free representation characterized by vivid express and bold outlines. In the later period the representation of fish was reduced to only one characteristic part of the aquatic animal, such as the head, body or caudal fin. The composite design of fish, human face and bird vividly reflected men's production activities and their aesthetic taste about 5,000 — 6,000 years ago.

人面魚紋彩陶盆（半坡）
Pot decorated with human face and
fish patterns (Banpo)

魚紋彩陶葫蘆瓶／部分（姜寨）
Calabash-shaped vase decorated
with fish pattern (part) (Jiangzhai)

網紋彩陶盆幾何紋彩陶缽（半坡）
Pot decorated with net pattern and bowl decorated with geometric designs (Banpo)

雙魚紋彩陶盆（半坡）
Pot decorated with double fish pattern (Banpo)

波紋彩陶罐（半坡）
Jar decorated with wave pattern (Banpo)

繩紋尖底瓶（半坡）
Vase with a pointed bottom,
decorated with cord pattern
(Banpo)

三角紋彩陶盆（半坡）
Pot decorated with triangular
designs (Banpo)

11

# 民間陶瓷
## POTTERY AND PORCELAIN

到了商代（公元前十六世紀——十一世紀）釉陶和初具瓷器性質的硬釉陶便已出現。魏晉時期（公元二二○年——四二○年）我國就已有了用高火度燒成胎質堅實的瓷器。唐代陶瓷的製作技術和藝術創造達到很高水平。明清時代的陶瓷從製坯、裝飾、施釉到燒成，技術上又有所發展。

陶與瓷的質地不同，性質各異。陶，是以粘性很高、可塑性強的粘土為主要原料製成，不透明、有細微氣孔和微弱的吸水性。瓷是以粘土、長石和石英製成，半透明、不吸水，胎質堅硬緊密。

陝西民間瓷窰遍及各地，以耀州瓷最負盛名（今銅川市），創燒於唐代，在北宋時期（公元九六○年——一一二七年）極為發達，是我國名瓷之一。耀瓷釉色以橄欖綠色為主，釉面透明度高，質地堅硬，時有冰裂，式樣雅樸，裝飾手法以刻花見長，間以梳齒紋樣，刻花剛勁有力，刀法洗練，綫條活潑流暢，疏密有致，紋飾題材豐富多樣，紋樣圖案濃淡分明，造型端莊、優美、古樸文雅。史書有"巧若范金，精比琢玉"之美譽。後燒白器，有似牛乳之白，其胎薄釉細，帶有暗花或青藍花，有簡練豪放、瀟灑自如的獨特藝術風格，呈自然異彩，光澤誘人。澄城堯頭瓷盛於清康熙年間，在黑釉瓷的民間日用器物上嵌以饒有情趣的花鳥、小動物形體，給人們一種欣然的生活樂趣。有的瓷呈黃灰色，極似出土的古瓷，釉光且潤。上面繪有人物、花卉等。

西安、莊里、延安、隴縣、雒南等地的陶瓷，有黑色、白色、茶褐色等，造型和花色都相繼在工藝上有所創新，渾厚大方，受到羣眾歡迎。

By the Shang dynasty (16th century BC — 11th century BC) glazed pottery and the hard glazed pottery that came near to porcelain had appeared. And by the Wei and Jin dynasties (AD 220—420) China had produced porcelain with a hard body fired at high temperatures. Both the techniques employed in manufacturing ceramics and artistic creation reached a very high level during the Tang dynasty. The Ming and Qing dynasties saw further technical progress in making the base, decorating, glazing and firing.

Pottery and porcelain are qualitatively different. Pottery is mainly made from the highly stickly and plastic clay; it is not translucent and is slightly porous and absorbent of water. Porcelain consists essentially of kaolin, quartz, and feldspar and is fired at high temperatures; it is semi-translucent, nonporous, nonabsorbent, hard and fine-grained.

Private kilns were found nearly everywhere in Shaanxi, but the best known of them was the one at Yaozhou (now the city of Tongchuan). One of the most famous varieities of Chinese porcelain, Yaozhou ware was first made during the Tang dynasty and attained a very high level of achievement in the Northern Song period (AD 960—1127). They have a hard body and an olive-green glaze, which is highly translucent and sometimes has fine crackles. The ware is particularly noted for its emphasis on simplicity of form and delicate incised decoration, combined sometimes with comb-tooth patterns. The incised designs show a sense of balance, are nearly executed, look forceful, and has a singular freedom of line. The motifs are varied, and the designs elaborate. They usually have a regular, graceful and antique shape. Some classical history books praise Yaozhou ware "as fine as gold-filled articles and as exquisite as jade carvings." The white porcelain manufactured later by the Yaozhou kiln has a thin-walled, milky-white body covered with clear glaze, and has designs lightly incised or painted in greenish-blue slip. It is unique also in its neat, bold and free artistic style and its rich natural colours which are very attractive.

The Yaotou ware of Chengcheng, which was popular in the reign of Emperor Kangxi of the Qing dynasty, is covered with a black glaze. They are usually decorated with floral, bird and other small animal designs. Some porcelain wares are yellowish-grey in colour, bearing a strong resemblance to the unearthed classic wares. They have a glossy and smooth glaze and are decorated with figural or floral motifs.

Ceramics produced in Xi'an, Zhuangli, Yanan, Long County and Luonan County show a great variety of colours, ranging from black, white to dark brown. They all are artifacts of innovative workmanship, and their simple and tasteful form and decoration are appealing to the common people.

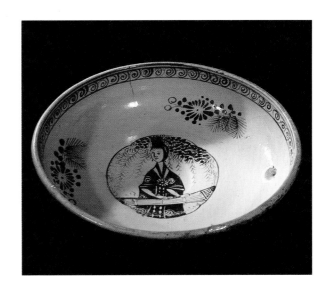

盤（澄城）
Plate (Chengcheng)

青瓷碗、壺（銅川）
Celadon bowl and pot (Chenlu, Tongchuan)

花釉花瓶（西安）
Vase decorated in coloured glazes (Xi'an)

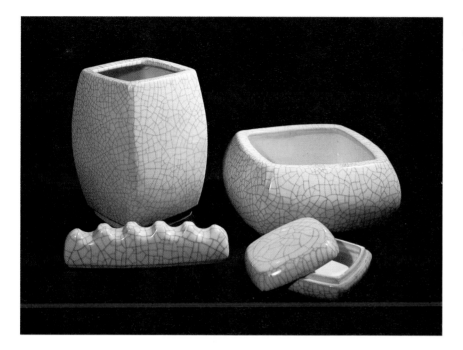

冰紋文房用品（西安）
Writing materials made of porcelain
with fine crackles (Xi'an)

色釉壺、罎（西安）
Glaze-coloured pot and jar (Xi'an)

黑剔花雜件（寶鷄）
Black sgraffito artefacts (Baoji)

剔釉巨馬花罇、龍紋梅瓶（西安）
Cut-glazed vessel with Juma floral decoration and plum-blossom vase decorated with dragon pattern (Xi'an)

青瓷梅瓶（銅川）
Celadon plum-blossom vase
(Tongchuan)

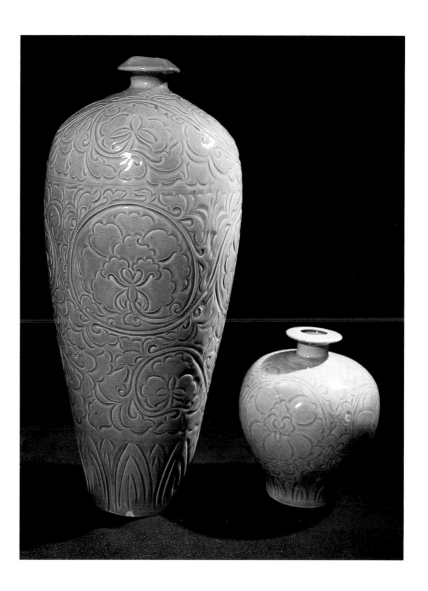

鐵綉花盤、蘭花碗（銅川陳爐）
Rust-coloured plate and orchid
bowl (Chenlu, Tongchuan)

# 拴馬樁石刻
# HITCHING POST

　　拴馬椿是陝西渭北農村拴系高脚子（骡、馬、驢）牲口的石頭椿子，椿頂一般都雕刻着特殊的各異的立體造像和浮雕紋樣，各色各目的人物，勾劃出社會生活的現實風貌，如骠悍豪放的獵手、氣勢咄咄的武士、沉穩幹練的牧人、热情殷勤的樂師、慈祥和善的老人、手捧雜果盤的長髮少女和稚態可掬的幼童等，其中可粗略辨識出來自不同地域、屬於不同族屬的人物形象。那威武凶悍的獅、活潑通靈的猴、枝蔓串卷的蓮花，寄寓着人們對牲畜蕃息、人丁興旺的願望祈求。

　　這些民俗石刻——莊戶人的"華表"，因材施藝，就坯取勢、自由靈活、想像豐富；整體造型渾厚簡練而重要部分細膩突出；善於誇張變型，追求內在的神態意趣。雕刻手法兼融多變，風格自然奔放，保留了漢唐遺風。人物造像詼諧、幽默，富於鄉野氣息和生命力。

　　在拴馬椿羣體中，其粗獷、自由，給人一種原始的混沌的美的感受，同時可覺察出多種不同時代藝術風格的痕迹，顯示出這種藝術的發展具有相當久遠的歷史跨度和時代延續性。

　　The hitching posts found in the countryside north of Wei River in Shaanxi Province are made of stone and their top parts are usually carved into various figures or patterns in bold relief. The sculptured figures include images of brave huntsmen, valiant warriors, experienced herdsmen, warm-hearted musicians, kind elders, young girls wearing long hair and holding trays full of fruits, and innocent children. Many of them can be dimly recognized as images of people coming from different regions and belonging to different nationalities. The powerful and fierce lion, the sportive and clever monkey, and the luxuriant lotus flowers and foliage embody the wishes of the people for a flourishing husbandry and a growing family.

　　These carved stone hitching posts are the "ornamental columns" erected in front of the peasants' houses. Art designs on them vary with different materials used and all show a luxuriant

imagination. They generally have a simple and vigorous form, with important parts carved out in graphic details. Exaggeration, distortion and many other techniques are employed to bring out the inner spirit and charm of the figures or objects. The natural and free artistic style bears the marks of the Han and Tang influences. The figures, usually in comic shapes, are full of the interest and vigour of rural life.

　　The boorish, bold and unconstrained style of such hitching posts produces a feeling of primitive beauty and shows traces of many artistic syles of different ages. This indicates that this folk type of art must have a long history and enjoy a continuous development.

# 皮 影
## SHADOW PLAY

皮影，是用牛皮或驢皮雕鏤繪製成影人、道具，通過燈光（油燈、汽燈、電燈）在影幕上透射，隨着劇情、唱腔、音樂伴奏而動作，表演出一定的故事情節來給人們觀賞的。

據史書記載，最早見於宋代。宋高承《事物紀原》記述："仁宗時，市人有能談《三國》事者，或采其說加以緣飾，作影人"。南宋吳白牧的《孟梁錄》中有"更有弄戲者，以皮雕形，用以色彩裝飾"。宋時影戲火完成了從"素紙雕鏤"到"彩色裝皮"的重要創造，形象上注意"公忠者雕以正貌，奸邪者刻以丑貌，蓋亦寓襃貶於其間耳"。元代初期，曾作爲軍隊內部的文娛活動，經常在軍營中流動演出。十三世紀初葉，傳入南亞各地，十八世紀中葉傳入歐洲。看來已有一千多年歷史了。世界各國的藝術家對我國皮影表現了濃厚的興趣。

皮影的美術造型獨具一格：既是一種圖案藝術，具有强烈的誇張性和濃厚的裝飾性，又是一種雕鏤藝術，運用洗練有力的雕刻綫條來塑造形象，結構畫面，這種藝術與民間窗花剪紙同出一源。皮影人物的造型及服飾又受到地方戲曲的影響，更臉譜化、程式化。羣衆稱讚它爲"隔紙說話"，影子抒情，一口述說千古事，雙手對舞百萬兵"。

陝西皮影分東路和西路兩大流派，西路體型高大，頭飾和身高一般在一尺以上，從頭到腿共十一部件，但都講究戲曲人物的造型美，注意刻劃人物性格和整體塊面效果，紋樣裝飾疏密相間，虛實有致。細處雕鏤精巧，粗處簡明概括，造型明晰。在人物形象處理上，生、旦、淨、丑和性格忠奸很易識别，相貌、衣着區别很大，平眉、皺眉、淨臉、花臉、大丑、小丑、老旦、靑旦等較秦腔臉譜更爲誇張，圖案性强，能充分體現人物性格。千姿百態，瑰麗多彩。

據有關專家根據一些史料推測："中國影戲之發源地爲陝西，自周秦兩漢以至隋唐當皆以其地爲最盛"。一致認爲它繼承了漢代畫像石質樸單純、富於裝飾性的傳統特點，以及宋代"院體畫"精致工麗的藝術風格。

Shadow play, called also shadow show, is a drama exhibited by throwing the shadows of puppets and props, usually cut from cattlehide or donkeyhide, on a screen through light (oil-lamp light, gas light or electric light).

According to historical records, shadow show first appeared during the Song dynasty. Gao Cheng of the Song dynasty made a note in his book *Original Records of Events*: "In the period of Renzong, there were town folks who could relate the story of the *Three Kingdoms* or develop the story and make it into a shadow play." Wu Baimu of the Southern Song said in his *Mengliang Records*: "Some theatrical performens cut leather into (human and various other) forms and decorate them in colour." The Song puppteers completed the important process from "cutting paper" to "colouring leather-silhouettes." And, in creating artistic images, they paid attention to "letting the impartial and faithful persons have good looks and the crafty and eveil persons havc ugly looks —— a means by which to imply their judgment on people." In the early period of the Yuan dynasty, shadow play was often put on in barracks as a kind of recreational activities of the soldiers.

Shadow play was introduced to South Asia in the early 13th century and then to Europe in the 18th century. It has a history of more than 1,000 years, and absorbs much interest of artists throughout the world.

The uniqueness of a shadow puppet lies in the fact that it is a work of both the highly exaggerative and decorative pattern art and the art of cutting. It has the same origin as paper-cutting. Shadow play figures and their costumes are influenced by local operas, but are more stereotyped and stylized. Some people describe shadow play as a drama in which "puppets talk across paper (screen), shadows express their emotion, one mouth can relate stories of thousands of years, and two hands can signal a million soldiers in fighting."

There are two schools of Shaanxi shadow play —— eastern and western. The western school is characterized by its comparatively larger puppet figures, which are usually 0.3m tall each, comprising 11 parts. But both schools stress the beauty of form of the puppets, the portraying of their character, and the overall dramatic effect. Decorations show a sense of balance. Some parts of the puppet are carved with precision, while others are simply executed, but taken as a whole, the figure has a clear-cut outline. Different types of characters in an opera, such as *sheng* (the male character type), *dan* (the female character type), *jin* (the "painted face" type of characters) and *chou* (clown), as well as their nature of being honest or wicked are readily distinguishable from their sharply different countenances and costumes. The facial make-up of the character types of *pingmei* (spread eyebrows), *zhoumei* (knited brows), *jinlian* (painted face), *hualian* (coloured face), *dachou* (literally, big clown), *xiaochou* (clown), *laodan* (old females), and *qingdan* (young women) is more exaggerated and patternized than Qinqiang, a local opera of Shaanxi. The different, colourful types of makeup can fully show the disposition of different characters.

Specialists deduce from historical records that "Chinese shadow play originates in Shaanxi, and it thrived in the privince more than any other places in the country during the Zhou, Qin, Western Han, Eastern Han, Sui and Tang dynasties." They also agree that the shadow play has retained the traditional characteristics of the Han stone tablets bearing engraved images —— simplicity and ornamentalism, and reflected the exquisite artistic style of the paintings of the Song imperial art academy.

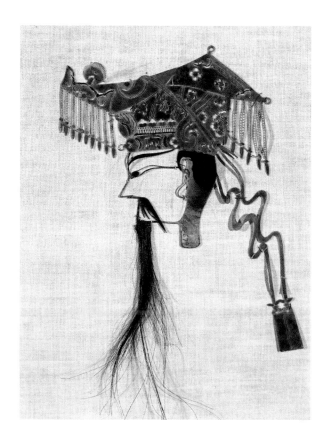

三鬚王頭
Thin-bearded king

大黑相
Black-faced Prime Minister

鳳
Phoenix

穆桂英
Mu Guiying

觀音菩薩
Guanyin Bodhisattva

秋娥（神戲人物）
Qiu-e (an opera character)

神妖
Goblin

鍘美案
The case of sentencing Chen
Shimei to death

車馬行人
Horse-drawn carriages and
pedestrians

小丑梳發官
Clown

# 木 偶
# PUPPETRY

　　木偶戲又名傀儡戲，最初脫胎於俑，在中國已有長遠歷史。據《列子湯問篇》記載，相傳在兩千多年前的殷周時代（周穆王）由名叫偃師的人創造的。以後的漢高祖至魏明帝時木偶能表演各種雜技，開始在宴會上演出（《唐書、音訓》"傀儡子，以偶作戲"）。敦煌莫高窟壁畫"弄皺"的形象，就是古代木偶表演的生動寫照。唐明皇曾寫過"刻絲木偶一老翁"的詩句。到了宋代有較大發展。中國戲曲的程式化，動作的舞蹈化，有種說法，就是來源於傀儡。

　　中國的木偶有豐富的劇種，這技藝苑奇葩深深植根於民間。現在比較流行的有杖頭木偶、提綫木偶、鐵枝木偶和布袋木偶。

　　杖頭木偶主要流行在陝西、甘肅等地，唱腔以秦腔爲主，不但善於表演傳統戲，而且能將傳統的操縱技巧應用到現代戲表演上。杖頭木偶是操縱者從下面用木杖撐起木偶進行表演，它的頭和身軀是空的（頭原是木雕的），沒有腿，衣服要能夠蓋住下半部，頭部現經藝人改進，有的已用紙殼在原模上托製，輕而方便，舉起後狀似葫蘆，所以關中農民又直呼木偶爲"肘葫蘆"。現在，陝西的木偶表演使杖頭、布袋、提綫幾種形式根據戲情需要綜合使用，整個造型優美、詼諧。有部分做成活動的，表演起來情趣橫生，引人入勝。

　　在農村以半職業性的農村民間藝人演出爲主。陝西木偶因在造型、製作、表演、舞美和音樂藝術上，尊重傳統技藝，又都有了創新的發展，生動逼眞，技巧精湛，加之唱腔優美，有醇郁的鄉土味，受到中外人士的歡迎。

　　木偶造型有它的"固定性"，臉部表情是固定不變的，只能顯示出一個角色單一的瞬間神態。木偶雕塑家就要在有限的瞬間裏，尋找豐富的意蘊。要高度提煉，旣要有性格，又要有裝飾美和高度誇張。

　　傳統的木偶造型，借鑒了民間神像、古代彩塑、石雕等的造型和技法，也吸收了戲曲臉譜的表現方法。木偶在神話戲的造型中，則特別見長，比眞人戲更優越，可以盡情的誇張塑造，盡可能地達到想像的程度。

Puppet play in China dates back to ancient times. According to *Liezi* (Chapter: Tang Wen), it was created by a person named Yan Shi in the reign of King Mu (Zhoumuwang) of the Zhou dynasty, more than 2.000 years ago. By the Han and Wei dynasties, puppets could be manipulated to perform acrobatics and were for the first time brought to the imperial palace to give shows during state banquets. (*Annals of the Tang Dynasty: Music Lecture:* "Puppets are used to stage a drama.") The image of "Nongzhou" in the murals in Dunhuang's Mogao grotto is a vivid depiction of the ancient puppet theatrical performance. A poem by Emperor Tang Minghuang of the Tang dynasty contains one line: "The woodcut puppet assumes the form of an old man." Puppet show made substantial progress during the Song dynasty. Some people say that the stylized movements in Chinese operas originate with puppet play.

There are many kinds of puppets. More popular among the people are rod puppets, string puppets, iron-rod puppets and glove puppets.

Rod puppets are especially popular in Shaanxi and Gansu Provinces, where the puppet theatres often offer Qinqiang opera. Rod puppets are suitable for performing not only traditional operas, but also modern drama.

Rod puppets are manipulated from below. These puppets have a hollow head and body. (The head is usually carved from wood.) Because they have no legs, their clothes have to be long enough to hide the lower part of the body. Now some of the puppets have a papier-mache head, and innovation introduced by the puppeteers. When the papiermache head is raised, it looks very much like a calabash and therefore, the peasants in the Guanzhong are often call this type of puppets "to elbow calabash." Now the Shaanxi puppet theatres tend to use all the three types of puppets —— rod, glove and string —— in a drama if it is called for by the story of the play. All the puppets are gracefully shaped, look humorous, and the whole performance is very interesting and charming. In the countryside the puppeteers are usually semi-professionals.

Shaanxi puppet theatres, while respecting traditional techniques, have introduced innovations in the making of puppets. Performance, dancing movements and music also have been improved. Puppets can skilfully and vividly portray life, and the music for voices is beautiful and has a strong local flavour. For all this they are much loved by both Chinese and foreign audience.

The puppet is characterized by its "fixity." For instance, a puppet has fixed facial expressions and is capable of presenting only one kind of momentary looks or moods. This characteristic of puppets requires that puppet sculptors try to give the figures the most meaningful type of expressions at a particular moment, impart them personality, and decorate them with beautiful designs while employing the method of exaggeration.

Traditional puppets are modeled after images of deities, ancient painted clay figurines and stone carvings. They also draw on the merits of the types of facial make-up in local operas. Puppets are at their best in performing mythological plays. They can act their parts better than actors, because they can be carved into various fantastic forms and manipulated to perform in a way the manipulator can conceive in imagination.

唐僧
Sanzang, the Tang Priest

孫悟空
Sun Wukong (Monkey)

猪八戒
Zhu Bajie (Pig)

沙和尚
Sha Wujing (Friar Sand)

鐵扇公主
Princess Iron Fan

牛魔王
The Demon King of Ox

**木偶戲《西遊記》**
Puppet show *Journey to the west*

**木偶戲的幕後操作**
Backstage manipulation of puppets

# 剪 紙
# PAPERCUTS

我國人民自古以來，就善於利用多種物質材料創造精美的藝術品，在製作中發現鏤空和透雕的美。原始社會以獸皮為衣時，便開始了穿孔打眼的活動，陶器、編織和玲瓏的牙、玉、骨等諸如此類器物的產生，培育了人們美的觀念和剪紙的意識。歷代諸工藝反映出來的異曲同工現象，證明了互相間派生關係和千絲萬縷的聯繫，向我們展示了剪紙形成、演變的脈絡關係。

在陝西農村，剪紙歷史悠久，極為普及，尤其在陝北、關中地區最盛，具有廣泛的羣眾性。每逢年節或喜慶婚事，農家都要換上新剪的各色窗花、炕圍花等（這也是姑娘、農婦們比心靈、比手巧的內容之一），與掛箋、對聯、彩燈交相輝映，把屋內屋外裝扮得花團錦簇，富麗飽滿，五彩繽紛！它給偏僻的山莊、簡樸的農家生活增添了歡樂的氣氛和盎然生機。

陝西剪紙題材內容廣泛，豐富多彩，形式多種多樣，有窗花、頂棚花、炕圍花、掛簾、門畫、枕花、鞋花等，窗花中又有轉花、雲子花、角花、煙格等，在連續圖案和單獨紋樣中，以傳統的吉祥如意的作品居多，各種人物、花鳥蟲魚、勞動果實、鎮邪惡的老虎、獅子，孳茸報春的鹿和家禽家畜等，還有不少是象徵寓意和諧音比喻的，如蓮與魚相配，作為"連子"隱語，是種族繁衍的歌頌，鴛鴦交頸、喜鵲鬧枝、石榴牡丹等，都有喜慶的雙關意思，又如吉慶有餘以戟磬有魚表示，用蝙蝠、鹿、鶴表示福、祿、壽等。總的看，陝西剪紙的藝術趣味充滿馥郁而純樸的生活氣息。

陝北剪紙風格古樸、凝煉、粗獷、渾厚，刀法洗練，綫條流暢，保留了漢代藝術那種蓬勃旺盛的生命力。延安一些窗花古中有古，一些人物造型和新石器時代彩陶上的舞蹈紋和漢畫像石相似，如傳統紋樣《抓髻娃娃》，在孩子的抓髻〔古人用"髻"作為婚配的象徵。〕上剪成雞形或兩隻飛鳥，考古學家說，這便是人類最早的圖騰標記。有的抓髻娃娃一手拿雞，一手托兔，雞屬陽，兔屬陰，意思是陰陽結合便有了生命。《蛇盤兔》意思是十二相中男屬蛇，女屬兔，表示家庭和睦，相親相愛，生活

富裕。《鶏壽童》它是祝福新婚夫婦，貼在洞房的禮花，有的突出男陰部位，並以牡丹花裝飾〔是從"生命"取義〕。《老鼠嫁女》是流傳甚廣的傳統窗花，詼諧、逗樂，有謂出於"除害宣傳"，據攷證，鼠為"子神"，當指十二辰"子鼠"，大約是作為繁育子孫的象徵。《茶壺和扣碗》也是作為"生命"的象徵而保留下來的傳統主題紋樣，看來，民間窗花剪紙和我國古老的民俗關係甚密，是民俗文化的血緣紐帶。

關中剪紙精細秀勁，注重裝飾美，結構嚴謹，風格典雅、明快，以鳳翔、岐山、周至、永壽、栒邑、三原等地尤為突出，有單色、套色、點染等多種藝術手法。

近年來，陝西剪紙已成為各地專家、學者研究中國西部美學、藝術史、民俗學的珍貴資料，對美術和工藝創作的民族化和推陳出新有寶貴的借鑒價值。

Since antiquity, the Chinese people have shown ingenuity in using various materials to create works of art. In such practices they found beauty in hollow-out objects. Even primitive men learned some skills of drilling and piercing, With the appearance of pottery, woven articles, and utensils made of tooth, jade and bone, people began to foster a sense of beauty and the conception of paper-cutting. The fact that all arts and crafts, though made in different ways, are equally satisfactory in result points to their close relationship and mutual influence, and enables us to determine the origin of paper-cutting.

Paper-cutting is a very old art in Shaanxi's countryside. It is expecially popular in the northern part of the province and Guanzhong area. On New Year or other festival days, such as wedding, every peasant home will put papercuts of all sorts on windows and the wall of *kang* (heatable adobe bed). The girls and young wives usually look paper-cutting on these occasions as a means to show their cleverness and deftness. And their products always add lustre to their homes, which are already decorated with lanterns and antithetical couplets written on two strips of red paper. Papercuts have brightened the simple life of the farmers in out-of-the-way villages.

Shaanxi papercuts are varied in both content and form. There are papercuts for decorating windows, ceilings, *kang*, screens, doors, pillowcases and shoes. Among the various window papercuts are *zhuanghua*, *yunzihua*, *jiaohua* and *yange*, just to name a few. For both serial and single papercuts, the most familiar motifs are those which augur good luck, including a variety of figural, floral and animal designs, such as bird, insect, fish, tiger, lion, dear, and domestic animals and fowls. Many of them are symbolic and often exploit the homonym or double meaning of certain Chinese words; for instance, lotus and fish put together mean "having many sons." Mating *yuanyang* (mandarin duck), Magpies and Plum Blossom, pomegranate and peony flowers are symbols of happiness. The combination of the designs of halberd, chime stone and fish represents *ji qing you yu*, or good luck, happiness and harvest with a surplus; and bat, dear and crane represent the three blessings —— good fortune, wealth and longevity. In terms of artistic taste, Shaanxi papercuts as a whole brim over with the vigour of simple rural life/

Northern Shaanxi papercuts are characterized by their unsophisticated, compact, bold and vigorous style, and their flowing lines illustrate great cutting skills. All this shows that they have inherited the vigorous style of the Han dynasty. Some figural designs in Yanan papercuts for window decoration resemble the patterns of dancing movements on the painted pottery of the Neolithic Age and the images on the Han stone tablets. One example is the traditional motif of "A Child with His Hair Worn in a Coil." The child's hair coil, a symbol of marriage in ancient times, is cut into the form of a cock or two flying birds, which, according to some archaeologists, is the earliest totemic sign of human beings. Sometimes the child holds a cock in one hand and a rabbit in the other, a design that means new life is born out of the combination of *yin* and *yang*, because the cock belongs to *yang* and the *rabbit, yin*. (In Chinese philosophy, *yin* represents the feminine or negative principle in na-

ture, while *yang*, the masculine or positive.) The design "Snake Twining Rabbit" indicates family harmony and affluence because the snake represents the male and the rabbit, the female.

The papercut with the "Cock and Child" design, which is to be put on the wall of the room of the newly wed, sometimes give prominence to men's private parts decorated with peony flowers, implying "life." "Mice Marry Their Daughter," a popular motif of papercuts for window decoration, is humorous, jocular. Some say the motif has been created to promote the campaign to eliminate "the pests," but others maintain that it symbolizes human reproduction because mouse is the "god of *zi*" and *zi*, the first of the 12 Earthly Branches, also means "son," while *shu* (mouse) is the first of the 12 animals representing the 12 Earthly Branches. Another traditional motife, "Teapot and Cup," is also a symbol of "life." These examples show that the papercuts for window decoration are closed related to China's old folk custom and constitute part of the popular culture.

The delicate Guanzhong papercuts are noted for their emphasis on beauty of decoration, compact composition and elegant style. Their outstanding representatives are those of Fengxiang, Qishan, Zhouzhi, Yongshou, Xunyi and Sanyuan. There are monochromic, chromatic, dip-dyed and other kinds of papercuts.

In recent years, Shaanxi papercuts have become an important source of information for experts to study West China's aesthetics, history of art and folklore. They can help Chinese artists to create works with Chinese characteristics.

蛇盤兔
Snake Twining Rabbit

石榴
Pomegrnate

虎（安塞）
Tiger (Ansai)

芯子（周至）
Wick (Zhouzhi)

獅子（鳳翔）
Lion (Fengxiang)

十二肖相（安塞）
The 12 Animals (representing the
12 Earthly Branches, used to
symbolize the year in which a
person is born) (Ansai)

老鼠娶親
A rat gets married

放牛（鳳翔）
Cowboy (Fengxiang)

老鼠偷食（千陽）
A mouse takes food on the sly
(Qianyang)

馬行車
Horse-drawn carriage

# 木版年畫
# NEW YEAR PICTURES

陝西木版年畫的歷史可追溯到公元十五世紀左右（明洪武時）。以關中鳳翔和陝南漢中爲主要產地。它繼承了我國繪畫和木刻雕版技法的優良傳統，題材內容豐富，形式多樣，綫條繁簡分明，遒勁有力，色彩誇張對比強烈，構圖集中概括，體現了農民羣眾的理想和質樸、健康、明朗的審美情趣。成爲一些地區農家春節前必備的"年貨"。它美化環境，增加節日氣氛，寄托着羣眾對幸福美滿的祈求，同時起着潛移默化的教育作用。

鳳翔木版年畫產地集中在縣城東面的南、北小里村和城西的陳村，有數百幅明清古版流傳至今，它從農民們的審美需要出發，以吉祥如意、鎮宅祛邪、健康平安、風調雨順、子孫繁衍、多福多壽、家庭和睦、生財有道、百業興旺、保衞家鄉、生產勞動等居多，即使那些表面上塗染了封建迷信色彩的神像，也莫不是祈求生活的安康，少受自然災害和社會災害的思想感情的反映。除了門畫外，還有相當一部分是反映傳統戲曲內容的戲曲歷史人物的配套版畫和描繪民情風俗、男耕女織和農家樂趣的，有濃郁的生活氣息，不少題材是採用民間習俗中的寓意和象徵手法來表現的。在傳世古版中，《小人圖》頗具諷刺意味，從八個側面抨擊了當時社會中八種丑惡行爲，發人深思。

漢中木版年畫，雄渾、莊重，具有中國民族藝術的神韵，是研究中國民間版畫史的珍貴資料。

民間版畫的形式有竪頁、橫頁、單頁、冊頁、連環畫、谷雨貼、四季條屏、中堂帶字條等，除了門神畫，還有窗扇畫、窰窩畫（四季花卉、倩女尋梅、佳人愛菊、多福多貴等），谷雨貼中包括十二生相、春牛圖、二十四節氣、八仙圖、單鷄雙鷄吃蝎子、張天師降五毒、胖娃娃、鎮宅伴子等，窗花畫中有四季果、鳥獸蟲魚、歷史戲劇人物等。鳳翔年畫中過去有種《金三裁》是通過單色變印，工筆重彩彩繪，套印鉛銀和工筆描金點妝，印染結合，色調層次分明，鮮艷奪目，濃淡協調，古雅、清麗。（三裁是指開數的尺寸，一張單膠紙三裁）木版年畫的色彩多用大紅、桃紅、大黃、深綠、鮮藍、墨、淡墨、紫色和縈色等水色，有濃厚的裝飾效果和民間藝術特色。

Shaanxi New Year pictures, colour prints made from engraved wood blocks, date from the 15th century, in the period of Hongwu of the Ming dynasty. Fengxiang in Guanzhong and Hanzhong in southern Shaanxi are the main producing areas of the prints.

Technically, Shaanxi New Year pictures are profoundly influenced by traditional Chinese painting and wood engraing. The painting generally shows powerful lines, either complicated or simple; presents sharp contrast between colours; and has a compact composition. All this typically reflects the peasants' ideals and their unsophisticated, healthy and bright aesthetic taste. Therefore, the picture are always among the peasants' special purchases for the Spring Festival, the Chinese lunar New Year. They serve not only to beautify the environment, add to the festive mood and express the peasants' wishes for a happy life, but also educate them in many things.

The chief producers of Fengxiang New Year pictures are South and North Xiaoli villages to the east and Cheng village to the west of the Fengxiang county seat, where several hundred wood blocks of the Ming and Qing dynasties are still being used. To meet the peasants' aesthetic taste, the dominant themes of the pictures are those expressing their desire for good luck, good health, favourable weather, a growing family, a long life, family harmony, fortunes, prosperity, driving out evil spirits, defending homeland, or showing production activities. Even though some pictures bear images of gods, thus smacking of superstition, they are but expressions of the peasants' wishes for a happy and secured life and fewer natural and social calamities.

A great number of Fengxiang New Year pictures, except the door pictures, feature traditional opera serials, folk customs or themes that peasants take delight in, such as "men engaged in tilling the land while women in weaving." Many of the designs are symbolic. One of the blocks handed down from the past is called "Portrayals of Mean Persons," which is a bitter satire exposing eight types of ugly human behaviour of that time.

Hanzhong New Year pictures appear to be forceful, vigorous and serious in style. They have the charm of traditional Chinese art and contribute valuable data to the study of the history of Chinese folk prints.

Wood-block printed New Year pictures assume varied forms. There are "vertical" and "horizonal" pieces (those for being hung up vertically or horizontally), monotypes, albums, series, Grain Rain pictures, four-season pictures, central scrolls (hung in the middle of the wall of the main room), etc. There are also door-god pictures, window pictures, and bedroom pictures which usually have floral designs or those showing pretty girls enjoy looking at plum flowers or chrysanthemum, or those symbolizing happiness. Grain Rain pic-

tures include those showing the twelve animals representing the twelve Earthly Branches (used to symbolize the year in which a person is born), cows, the 24 solar terms, the Eight Immortals, cocks pecking at scorpions, Heavenly Master Zhang vanquishing the five demons, chubby babies, and household gods. Among the window pictures are some that show fruits of the four seasons, birds, beasts, insects, fish, or figures in historical drama.

There used to be a Fengxiang New Year picture called "Golden *sancai*." (*sancai* means a sheet of offset paper cut into three parts.) It was chromatographed and traced in gold. The bright colours harmonized perfectly and the whole picture looked elegant and beautiful.

Shaanxi New Year pictures usually use bright red, peach-blossom, bright yellow, dark green, dark blue, black, light black, purple, dark redish brown and other water colours. These colours, typical of works of folk art, have strong ornamental effects.

吉慶有魚（鳳翔）
Enough happiness and to spare
(Fengxiang)

女十忙（鳳翔）
Ten women's jobs
(Fengxiang)

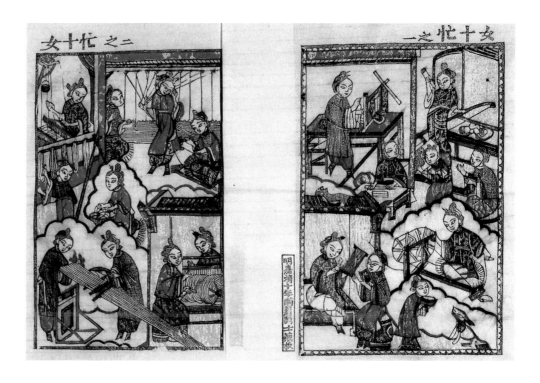

四時報喜（鳳翔）
Four-Season Greetings pictures
(Fengxiang)

大幅門神（漢中）
A large door-god picture
(Hanzhong)

魚樂圖之一（鳳翔）
Happy fishing (part of a serial)
(Fengxiang)

小人圖（鳳翔）
Portrayals of mean persons
(Fengxiang)

唐代英雄人物秦瓊（鳳翔）
Qin Qiong, a hero of the Tang
dynasty (Fengxiang)

回荊州之一（鳳翔）
Return to Jingzhou —— part of a
serial (Fengxiang)

唐代英雄人物敬德（鳳翔）
Jing De, a hero of the Tang
dynasty (Fengxiang)

# 泥玩具
## CLAY TOYS

陝西的彩繪泥塑玩具主要產地在鳳翔縣城東的六道營村，農閒時（尤其每當春節來臨之際），大部分人家都製作泥塑玩具，近年來有不少泥玩具專業戶，出售給四鄉人們作爲互相贈送的禮品。

這些彩繪泥塑玩具，在我國民間藝術中風格獨特，造型優美，生動逼眞，活潑可愛，已成爲雅俗共賞的鄉土藝術品。它的歷史相傳起於六百多年前的明代。內容有神話及歷史人物（唐僧、孫悟空、猪八戒、八仙、西遊記等）、動物（虎、獅、牛、馬、猪、狗、鷄、駱駝等）和植物瓜果等，多是空心的圓塑體，也有浮雕式的掛片，如虎頭、孫悟空、麒麟送子、福祿壽、劉海戲金蟾等）。

泥玩具製作簡便，由匠師先捏製模型，用當地的粘土和紙漿攪拌成塑泥，按模翻製胎坯，晾乾修飾，再泥坯罩粉，墨勾彩繪，最後清漆上光。

鳳翔泥玩具造型概括、洗練，能抓住對象特徵，删繁就簡，表現出描繪對象的內在性格，進行變形處理，追求寫意的藝術效果。如常見的泥虎，虛構合理、誇張適度、變形得法，它不是老虎自然形態的模擬，它概括了虎、獅、豹共有的凶猛性格，扭曲了虎的原形，把虎的身軀和尾巴都大幅度收縮了，老虎的四肢也極度的簡化，可是老虎的主要特徵却絲毫沒有丟掉，虎的頭部更給予着意的刻劃，眼睛、嘴巴都突出地加以誇張，使其成爲一個生氣勃勃、穩健强壯的五顏六色的可愛的玩具老虎，這也就是我國傳統藝術講究的"不肖形似，而求神似"吧，這樣的老虎形象是把現實和幻想中的虎交融在一起，並賦予它們人的性格和感情。在色彩上它捨棄了生活的眞實，極力追求藝術的眞實，採用了强烈、明快、鮮艷的對比色調，有飽和、跳躍的視覺效果；還有大方純樸、憨厚可親的黑牛和驃悍的馬等，都達到了形神兼備的境界。嬰兒滿月，外婆舅舅必購老虎座偶或麒麟送子相贈，以示祝福，它也是爲孩子驅邪的護衞者。

鳳翔泥玩具用色以大紅、大綠和黃爲主。酣暢的綫條和簡練的筆法塗染的浪漫而神奇的紋飾，使人感到明快醒目，散發着泥土氣香。

西安魚化寨和狄寨燒製的泥哨（泥叫叫），高六、七公分，頭部和背後有兩個小孔，可吹響。造型簡練，突出形象特徵，多以傳統戲曲人物和歷史神話人物爲主，是關中民間小地攤上賣的一種小耍貨，能觀賞、能吹響。

在榆林、蒲城、乾縣等地也有少量泥玩具生產，風格各異。榆林萬家的泥塑注重逼眞寫實，典雅自然。蒲城、乾縣的泥娃娃掛片、圓塑，粉底上少施點染，拙中見巧，生動有趣。

據陸游《老學庵筆記》載：宋時陝西鄜州田化以所製泥孩姿態無窮而馳名。看來，歷史較爲久遠。

Shaanxi's painted clay toys are mainly produced in Liudaoyin village to the north of the Fengxiang county seat. In leisure time, expecially in the period before the Spring Festival, most households in the village are engaged in making clay toys. Recent years have seen the emergence of many households specialized in this industry. They sell their products to people of neighbouring villages, who would send them to others as gifts.

Among the Chinese folk arts, the painted clay toys are unique in their style. They are beautifully shaped, vivid, lively and lovely. They have become an art that is appealing to both the elite and the unsophisticated.

The history of the painted clay toys goes back to the Ming dynasty, more than 600 years ago. Popular themes include mythical and historical figures: Sanzang (the Tang Priest), Monkey (Sun Wukong) and Pig (Zhu Bajie), all leading characters in the novel *Journey to the West*; and the Eight Immortals, animals: tiger, lion, cow, hourse, pig, dog, chicken, camel, etc., as well as fruits. The toys usually have a hollow body. Some are flat sculptures, such as the tiger's head; the image of Sun Wukong; Chinese unicorn bringing a son to you; designs symbolic of happiness, wealth and longevity; and Liu Hai playing with the Gold Toad.

The process of making such clay toys is not complicated. The artisan will first make a model, then make roughcasts after the model by using a misture of clay and pulp, which are to be sun-dried, powdered, painted, and finally varnished.

Fengxiang clay toys usually do not copy the forms of the objects they depict. In shape they resemble them only in a general manner. Often simply but neatly moulded, they try to represent only the salient features of familiar animals or popular objects, with more interest in the idea than in the representation itself. Therefore, the method of distortion or deformation is widely employed. For example, the familiar clay tiger is not a blind imitation of the real tiger, but incorporates the characteristic features of tigers, lions and leopards in itself. The body and tail of the tiger would be considerably reduced, and the legs simplified. But the head is sculptured with meticulous care, and the eyes and mouth are greatly exaggerated. Through such proper exaggeration and distortion of the natural form of the tiger, the effect is that you have a vigorous, powerful, colourful and lovely toy tiger. This method is typical of traditional Chinese art which "does not seek a resemblance in form but a resemblance in spirit" of what it represents. In terms of image, the toy tiger is a combination of the real tiger and the imaginary tiger. It has been personified.

In the use of colour, Fengxiang clay toys do not copy life either. Instead, they try to reflect the artistic reality. They prefer using bright colours and tend to bring the contrast between them into such clear relief that will give a saturation and bouncing visual effect. Apart from the toy tiger, the black clay cow and horse also reach a high artistic level —— they resemble the real animals not only in form but also in character. When a baby is a month old, its grandmother-in-law or its mother's brothers surely will give it a clay toy tiger or a "Unicorn-Brings-You-a-Son" toy as a gift. The toy will serve the baby both as a plaything and a talisman.

Fengxiang clay toys are often painted in bright red, bright green and yellow. The romantic, miraculour designs in flowing lines give them a bright, cheerful and lively look and send out the fragrance of country life.

The clay whistles (called *nijiaojiao* by the local people) produced in Yuhua village and Di village near Xi'an often take the form of historical or mythical figures or characters in traditional operas.

About 6–7 cm long and with two holes on the head and the back each, these finely made clay whistles are always available on the open markets in Guanzhong area.

Yulin, Pucheng and Qian Counties also produce some clay playthings of varied styles. The clay sculptures made by the Wan family of Yulin are characterized by their realistic representation of objects, looking elegant and natural. The flat clay figurines of Pucheng and Qian Counties, usually decorated with simple designs, show ingenuity in clumsiness.

According to Lu You, a poet of the Song synasty, Tianhua in Fuzhou, Shaanxi, was famous for its clay figurines in endless forms in the Song synasty. (See his *Notes Made in Laoxue Temple*.) It seems that Shaanxi clay toys have a very long history.

大座虎（鳳翔）
Sitting tiger (Fengxiang)

福祿壽三星（榆林）
The Three Stars: Happiness,
Wealth and Longevity (Yulin)

李白踏雪尋梅（榆林）
Li Bai enjoys looking at plum
blossom in the snow (Yulin)

白馬與松鼠（鳳翔）
Horse and squirrel (Fengxiang)

獅子（鳳翔）
Lion (Fengxiang)

娃騎犟牛（鳳翔）
Cowboy (Fengxiang)

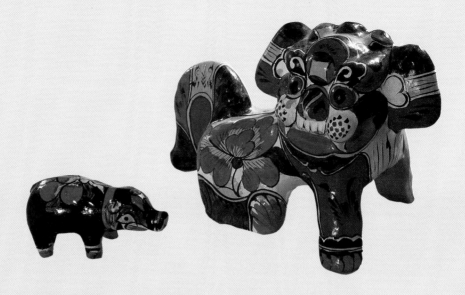

獅子與小猪（鳳翔）
Lion and piglings (Fengxiang)

卧牛與小狗（鳳翔）
Cow and doggie

# 布製玩具
# TOYS MADE OF CLOTH

慧心巧手的村姑農婦們，用平時做衣裳剪裁剩下的各種布頭，經過一番藝術想像的再創造，通過剪、綉、貼、拼，用彩綫作出一件件饒有情趣的鄉土藝術品，那威武逗人的布老虎最爲普及，還有虎頭、猪頭鞋帽、布娃娃、布猴、布鷄、布獅、布貓、布狗等，凝聚着勞動人民對生活的熱愛，傾注了生活的激情和質樸美的追求，她們像是要把整個世界都變成藝術品，與民間習俗禮儀尤爲密切，這是架設在長輩與兒孫之間傳遞愛的暖流的最初的橋。

外孫滿月時，外婆要把自己親手做的布老虎送去，這美麗奇特的禮物齜牙瞪眼，然而它渾身花朶，又顯得可愛！這是勞動者一種嚴謹的審美意識的產物。它的威風和震懾力說明它是外孫的守護神，它的壯觀和美麗可愛又符合兒童的審美心理，不失爲孩子的忠實朋友。在羣衆的審美中，老虎是作爲勇猛端祥的象徵，"虎"成了威武雄壯的代名詞，美好的代名詞，其內容，遠遠超出了虎的本身，給孩子起乳名有叫小虎子，寓意健壯有活力的心願。在關中，民間有種習俗：外孫成年結婚後，外孫媳婦用布做一隻雄鷄，鷄身綉上花卉，等給外公（或外婆）拜壽時作爲禮品送去，祝長者長壽。事後，這個壽鷄就成了外公一生珍藏的"無價之寶"；去世時還要把壽鷄放在棺內，讓雄鷄引路，使其靈魂升天。

布玩具在民間有許多傳統樣式，有擺件、掛件之分。一般採取簡潔明瞭的表現手法，形式簡約，刻意傳神。蘊藏着祈望幸福、美滿、歡樂、健康、興旺的思想感情。從中可悟到質樸而又奧妙的"鄉土美學"。

The country maids and young women in Shaanxi always like to make something out of tailor's clippings or other odd bits of cloth in their leisure time. And their such efforts often result in an interesting work of art, or folk art, that takes much creative imagination and a lot of cutting, embroidering, patching and needling to create. The most popular of their creations is cloth tiger, and next are tiger's head, cloth shoes, caps in the shape of pig's head, dolls, chickens, lions, cats, dogs, etc. Crystalized in all these playthings is their love of life and their longing for the beautiful. They would like, it seems, to transform the whole world into a work of art.

Cloth toys have much to do with folk custom. When an infant is a month old, its grandmother-in-law will give it a cloth tiger handmade by herself. The gift, though baring its teeth and opening its eye wide, is actually very lovely because it is painted in beautiful floral designs. It is a product of the labouring people's aesthetic ideas. Its militant bearing and awe-inspiring look tell people that it is the baby's god of protection, while its magnificance and loveliness, which meets children's aesthetic psychology, makes it a loyal companion of the infant. In folk art, tiger is seen as a symbol of courage, and the word "tiger" is a synonym for power and prestige; indeed, it is a synonym for everything beautiful and good. So, its implications are far beyond what it denotes literally. When a boy is given the name "Little tiger," it is hoped that he will grow strong and be full of vigour.

It is the folk custom in Guanzhong that when a young man gets married, his wife will make a cloth cock embroidered with flowers and present it to her grandfather-in-law (or grandmother-in-law) on his birthday. The grandfather will keep this gift —— cock of longevity —— all his life and will have it buried with him when he died, in the hope that the cock will lead his soul to Heaven.

Cloth playthings come in various shapes and forms, but traditionally they are divided into two types: those for being displayed on desks or shelves, and those for being hung on walls. Usually simply made, but always highly expressive, they serve to illustrate popular subjects embodying the labouring people's wishes for happiness, good health and prosperity. From them one get some idea of the simple and profound "rural aesthetics."

虎（西安）
Tiger (Xi'an)

布虎（西安）
Tiger (Xi'an)

獅子舞綉球（鳳翔）
Lion sporting with an ornamental
ball (Fengxiang)

布虎（西安）
Tiger (Xi'an)

虎子（西安）
Tiger (Xi'an)

魚枕（鳳翔）
Pilow in the form of fish (Fengxiang)

魚枕（西安）
Pillow in the form of fish (Xi'an)

戴帽花猴（鳳翔）
Capped monkey (Fengxiang)

貓壁掛（鳳翔）
Cat (a wall hanging)
(Fengxiang)

雙頭驢（西安）
Two-head donkey
(Xi'an)

蓮生貴子壁掛（陝北）
Lotus and boy —— a wall hanging
(Shanbei)

蓮生貴子壁掛（陝北）
Lotus and boy —— a wall hanging
(Shanbei)

娃娃魚與鯉魚（鳳翔）
Giant salamander and carp
(Fengxiang)

# 刺　繡
# EMBROIDERY

中國刺繡的歷史十分悠久，湖南長沙馬王堆漢墓出土的"長壽繡"、"信物繡"表明，早在兩三千年前，繡品已達到相當水平，晉代王嘉《拾遺記》中說："三國時期，吳主趙夫人能刺繡作列國圖，方帛之上，寫以五岳河海行陣之形，時人謂之針絕"，此爲我國刺繡作畫之最古者。《孔雀東南飛》中有"妾有繡腰襦，草莽自生光"的描述。唐朝詩人胡令能還曾專門作"咏繡障"詩："日暮堂前花蕊嬌，爭拈小筆上床描。繡成安向小園裏，引得黃鶯下柳條。"明代，葡萄牙商人從中國購得一批繡片攜歸，受到國王上賞，從此，我國繡品播譽世界各地。

陝西民間刺繡繼承了我國的傳統工藝，從款式、圖案組織和形象、色彩變化上都顯示出很大的豐富性和獨特的藝術個性，展示了巧婦閨秀們的巧手美思。

至今沿習不衰的是在傳統婚俗裏和大量兒童服飾上的刺繡裝飾，在洞房中可看到姑娘們在出嫁前用幾年功夫精心製作的各種繡品。做工精細講究，圖案新巧的花鞋墊，成爲閨秀和新娘寄托情思的"信物"，有的在圖案中套上工整的"正字"，這是要求戀人走正路的高尚情操的示意。那繡滿吉慶圖案方（圓）繡花枕，是年輕女子必備的嫁妝。兒童服飾上的刺繡紋樣，飽含着長輩對孩子的良好祝願，爲孩子驅除邪惡，納福求祥，四季安康。姑娘們作爲嫁妝的繡花枕以"魚戲蓮"、"蓮花石榴"、"鳳凰牡丹"、"喜鵲鬧梅"等爲主。孩子用的動物枕多用彩色布料製作，形象生動，別具一格。有的在枕的中心，還挖空一個耳窩（耳枕），幼兒睡眠時耳朵放在裏面不受壓，可起保護作用，真可謂匠心獨運！繡花肚兜是民間一種保暖衣飾，較流行的"五毒肚兜"是給孩童用的，繡的青蛙、蛇、蝎子、蜈蚣、蜘蛛（或壁虎、土元），五種民間認爲有毒的動物形象，基本布局是形體最大的青蛙居中，四周繡上其它幾種，有的爲追求逼真作成浮雕形，祝願兒童健康成長。

民間刺繡有幾十種不同針法，熔畫理與刺繡於一爐。色彩明快，層次清楚，反映了西北人民淳樸樂觀的性格和多姿多彩的生活習俗。

陝西刺繡落針用綫無痕迹，畫與針法渾爲一體。針法有暈針、切針、拉針、沙針、挑針等多種，其特點是平、齊、細、密、勻、順，短針細密，針脚平齊，片針光亮，紋理分明。借助各色粗細不同的絲綫，利用針法的巧妙，綫色的光澤，表現出五彩繽紛的圖景。

千陽、洛川縣近年創新的"毛繡"，樸中見巧，造型上不拘泥於生活的表象，它是選用粗麻包布作底，用粗毛綫引繡，吸取民間剪紙、年畫、民族圖案的特點，造型誇張，用色大膽，被譽爲中國的"新壁掛"，在展銷中引起工藝美術界的矚目。

西安古城的穿羅繡也以它的清秀典雅，獨具風采，受到中外人士的讚賞。

挑花、架花，流行在陝南秦巴之間的漢中盆地，內容豐富，針法工雅，圖案精巧，含情深切。它的用途最適合於小件繡品的邊花，如領口、袖口、褲脚、裹腿及手巾、枕巾、包單、床圍、門簾、帳簾、抬布等上的邊花及角花，或在游花中和其它針法摻合作爲填充圖案，在陝南已逐漸形成了一整套的組合繡品的圖樣及格式。它是依平布經緯綫路，朝左右兩個方向平行運行針法，針碼可按圖樣的需要，有長有短，產生的花紋正面和背面一陰一陽，深淺變化相反，多爲二方連續或均衡的圖案組織，有團花、方花、樹花、瓶花、盆花、花籃及其它人物景物等。樸實、耐用、美觀，是一種變形美術。

Chinese embroidery boasts a very long history. As the "Longevity embroidery" and "Token embroidery" unearthed from the Mawangdui Han Tomb in Changsha, Hunan Province, indicate, it reached a rather high level of development some 2,000–3,000 years ago. Wang Jia of the Jin dynasty wrote in *Making Good Omissions*: "In the period of Three Kingdoms, Madame Zhao, wife of His Lord the Chief of Wu, could embroider the map of all kingdoms on a piece of silk fabric, with the mountain ranges, rivers and sees all clearly shown. People of that time described it as superb needle-work." The said map was perhaps the earliest recorded embroidery in China.

*Peacock Flies Southeast*, an ancient Chinese poem, contains the two lines:"I have an embroidered waistcoat, its lush floral designs radiant." Hu Ling, a poet of the Tang dynasty, wrote a poem entitled "Ode to the Embroidered Screen," which reads: "The flowers in front of the hall look charming at sunset, and the girls are vying to depict them on silk. When the embroidering finished and in the garden the piece displayed, coming down from the willow trees are orioles attracted." During the Ming dynasty, some Portugese businessmen came to China and bought some embroideries, and when they returned home with these embroideries they were highly awarded by their king. Since then Chinese embroidery has become well-known throughout the world.

Shaanxi embroidery has inherited traditional Chinese embroidery techniques. It also shows great richness and artistic distinction in style, design and the use of colour.

Embroideries are commonly seen at weddings. In a bridal chamber one can see various embroidered articles that took the bride several years to make before marriage. The finely embroidered shoe-pads are tokens of the bride's love. In their floral pattern is sometimes embroidered the Chinese word for "right," implying that the bride wants her lover to take a "right" road. The pillowcase embroidered with auspicious patterns symbolic good luck are a necessary dowry.

Children's clothes are usually embroidered with designs that give expression to parents' best wishes for their sons or daughters, whishes for their happiness, health and not being haunted by eveil spirits. With regard to embroidered pillowcases used as a dowry, the motifs are mostly "Carps Under the Lotus Flowers," "Lotus Flowers and Pomegranate," "Phoenix and Peony Flowers," and "Magpies and Plum Blossom." Children's pillows are usually made of pieces of cloth of a variety of colours and in the form of animals. Sometimes the pillow has a hollow part in the middle in the shape of ear, which can hold the baby's ear when it sleeps on its side with its head resting on the pillow, thus protecting the ear from being pressed and hurt. What ingenuity it is!

Embroidered *dudou* (literally, belly-cover) is an apron-shaped underwear worn by the rural people to keep warm. The most familiar of them is the Children's "five-poisonous-animal *dudou*," which is embroidered with frog, snake, scorpion, centipede and spider (or house lizard), the five animals that the country folks consider poisonous. The big frog is sually put in the centre, surrounded by the other four animals. Sometimes all the five animals are embroidered in bold relief to seek the effect of vivid representation. The idea is to wish children healthy growth.

Shaanxi embroidery is particularly noted for its exquisite workmanship. Executed in fine close stitches, it looks smooth, neat and glossy, The stitches are hardly visible. The clever use of thick and thin colour silk threads and a rich variety of stitches guarantees its superb quality.

Qian Yang and Luo Chuan have in recent years created a kind of woolwork which shows ingenuity behind clumsy appearance. The embroidery is done in thick knitting wool on burlap, and adapts patterns typical of popular papercuts and New Year pictures for its own artistic purpose. Exaggerated in style and bold in the use of colours, the embroidery is reputed to be China's "new-type wall hangings," arousing great interest in the arts and crafts circles.

The *chuanluo* embroidery produced in Xi'an is will-known for its distinctive, elegant style and has won praise from many people, both Chinese and foreigners.

Cross-stitch work is popular in Hanzhong Basin in southern Shaanxi. They boast a great variety of motifs, fine stitches and delicate patterns. They are best suited to decorate laces, collars, wristbands, bottoms of trouser legs, puttees, towels, towels used to cover pillows, wrappers, bedspreads, door curtains, tablecloth and other petit embroidered articles. They also can be used as fill-ins of other ebroiderery patterns. They are executed on plain cloth by stitching parallel right and left along the warp and weft threds of the cloth. The stitches can be small or long depending on the design used. And the usually floral designs, which are visible on both sides of the cloth but of different shades of colour, take a variety of shapes —— round, square or tree-like. There are also designs of vases, pots and baskets of flowers and figural designs.

Cross-stitch work shows simplicity of beauty and is durable. It is unique type of fine arts.

秦綉文成公主（西安）
Qin embroidery with the portrait of
Princess Wencheng (Xi'an)

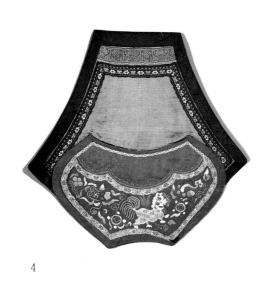

1 蝶花背心（澄城）
Vest embroidered with butterflies and flowers (Chengcheng)

2 獅子圍咀（渭南）
Bib embroidered with a lion (Weinan)

3 虎頭帽（渭南）
Cap in the form of a tiger's head (Weinan)

4 綉花肚兜（澄城）
Embroidered dudou (belly-cover) (Chengcheng)

5 雜耍肚兜（澄城）
Dudou (belly-cover) embroidered with jugglers (Chengcheng)

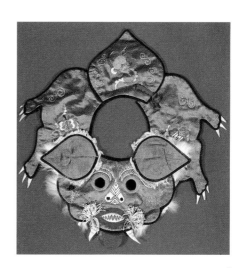

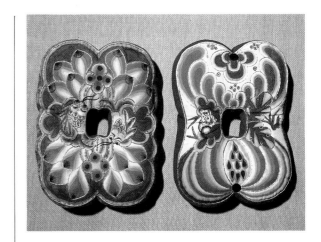

1

2

1 繡花枕頂（澄城）
Embroidered pillowslip
(Chengcheng)

2 耳枕（渭南）
Ear Pillow (Weinan)

3 套袖（澄城）
Oversleeves (Chengcheng)

4 繡花披肩（澄城）
Embroidered shawl (Chengcheng)

5 鞋墊（寶鷄）
Shoe-pads (Baoji)

3

4

5

# 印染花布
# COTTON PRINTS

　　藍印花布，是相傳久遠又是目前農村、城市較流行的富有鄉土氣息和中國民族特色的質樸大方的棉質印染品。

　　這種花布由於生產工具簡便，只用一套色彩，手工操作，色澤經久不變，清新淳樸，為農家習用。它的花紋一般採用人們喜聞樂見的吉祥題材，創造出富有變化而又和實用密切結合的圖案。它一般是用油紙刻版，由於紙面的限制，綫條不能互相連續，只能用短的斷綫、點子或大塊大面的花形來表現花紋形象，有白底藍花和藍地白花兩種，一般用作門簾、被面、床單、圍腰、包袱皮、頭巾等。

　　彩印花布多用作包袱皮、桌簾，是在白布或淺色布上用三、四種色彩套印而成，絢麗多彩而又散發着泥土芳香。

　　以上兩種花布多以鴛鴦荷花、魚戲蓮來象徵夫妻和睦、連生貴子、年年有餘，以佛手、桃、松鶴象徵多福多壽，以鳳凰牡丹象徵富貴等，在門簾上還配有貼題的對聯、橫額題字裝飾，構圖飽滿，表達了人們嚮往美好的情感。

　　在我國西北地區，曾發現過漢、晋和唐朝的一些印染遺物，有的就是較單純的藍地白花，也有的是用多種色彩印成的。到了宋代，有種"藥斑布"，是"以灰藥塗布染青，俟乾拭去，青白成圖，有山水、樓台、人物、花果、鳥獸諸象"。這些都是民間印花布的歷史軌跡。

　　扎染，是將布、綢、紗用多變的綫繩捆扎後，經過深淺不等的多色的巧妙蘸染（要根據事先設想的構成圖樣），就顯現出多種互不相同變化萬千的拙樸典雅的自然花紋，適用於衣裙、頭巾等。

　　格子條紋土布，遍及農村，是民婦在土織布機上通過多彩的經緯綫層次變化創造的藝術品，以色綫有規律的交替使用而成，格式根據各地習俗多種多樣，渾厚樸實，婦女、兒童衣物多採用。

Blue cotton prints have long been, and still are, very popular in town and country. Typically Chinese, they display the beauty of rustic simplicity.

Peasants like this cotton prints. It can be made with simple tools and its colour can be permanently kept. It is usually decorated with auspicious patterns that are appealing to the common people. The patterns, cut on oilpaper, are usually made up of only broken lines or dots or large floral designs because of the limited size of the oilpaper. There are mainly two kinds of the cotton prints: one with blue decorations on a white ground and the other with white decorations on a blue ground. Both are usually used for door curtains, quilt covers, bed sheets, aprons, wrappers and scarfs.

Multicoloured cotton prints are usually used for wrappers and tablecloth.

Decorations are highly symbolic; for instance, mandarin ducks and lotus flowers, or carps and lotus flowers, symbolize harmony between husband and wife, many sons and bumper crops with surplus every year. Fingered citron (Buddha's-hand), peach, or pine tree and crane, represent happiness and longevity; and phoenix and peony flowers symbolize wealth. The door curtain is sometimes decorated with couplets or other inscriptions in Chinese expressing people's aspirations for a better life.

Some dyed fabrics of the Han, Jin and Tang dynasties have been found in northwestern China, and some of them are cotton prints with white designs on a blue ground or multicoloured cotton prints. By the Song dynasty, a sort of "cloth with blotches" appeared. It was made by applying a coat of a grey chemical powder on calico, which was then dyed in blue. When the cloth dried, the chemical powder was wiped off it, and the white designs would appear on the blue cotton print, showing landscapes, pavilions, figures, flowers, fruits, birds or other animals.

What may be called "bundle dyeing" refers to the dyeing process in which some plain cloth, silks and cotton yarn are bundled up in different manners and dip-dyed successively in different colours in a way as required by the preconceived pattern. The result is a great variety of natural patterns in different forms. Such dyed fabrics are good materials for making skirts and shawls.

The home-spun checked and striped cloth varies from place to place in both style and designs on it, but, whatever places it is made, it is finely woven from coloured cotton threads at the country women's loom. The thick, plain-looking cloth is usually for women and children garments.

藍印花布包袱皮（澄城）
Blue cotton cloth wrapper
(Chengcheng)

藍印花門簾（澄城）
Door curtain made of blue cotton
prints (Chengcheng)

65

彩印包袱（澄城）
Wrapper made of chromatically
printed cloth (Chengcheng)

魚戲蓮彩色包袱皮（澄城）
Multicoloured cotton cloth wrapper
with the motif of "Carps under the
lotus Flowers" (Chengcheng)

魚戲蓮彩色包袱皮（澄城）
Multicoloured cotton cloth wrapper with the motif of "Carps under the
lotus Flowers" (Chengcheng)

民間土格子布（寶鷄）
Homespun checked fabrics (Baoji)

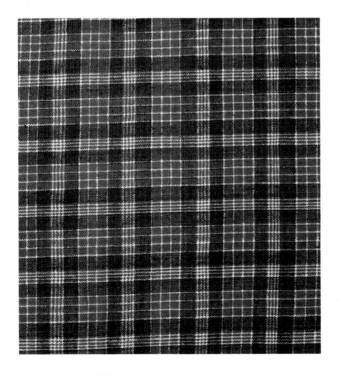

民間格子布（寶鷄）
Checked fabrics (Baoji)

扎染頭巾（西安）
Scarf made of "bundle-dyed"
cloth (Xi'an)

扎染（西安）
"Bundle dyeing" (Xi'an)

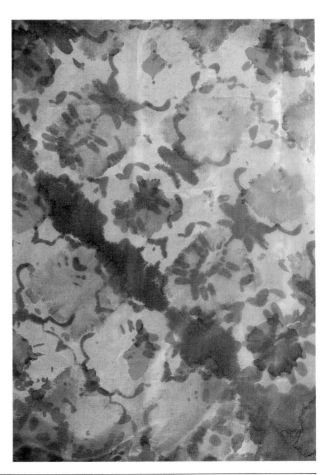

# 香 包
# PERFUME POUCH

端午節，民間有許多傳統習俗，縫製香包就是其中之一。香包，又叫荷包、香囊、香袋等。相傳遠古人在狩獵時為免遭毒蟲傷害，在身邊裝些草藥包，現在，有些老年人終年掛着形似葫蘆的香袋，似乎就是這一藝術來源的足迹。又相傳，屈原於農曆五月初五投汨羅江而死。當時秦楚相連，秦地人民出於同情、懷念，按照屈原生前喜愛芳草、香料的夙願，做香包戴在身邊。又說這是唐代以來漢族就有的習俗。在農家，每年農曆四月，農村巧婦便忙着用彩色絲綢、花絲綫、金銀彩珠等，裁剪縫製。到了清代，戴香包就不限於端午節了。原來滿族也有佩戴香包的風俗，按清朝規矩，帝、后們要常年佩戴香包，每至歲暮或四時八節，皇帝還要按例賞賜各王公大臣香包，以示眷寵。更有趣的是連同治和光緒選擇皇后，也用香包：待選的姑娘排成行，由皇帝挑選，看中誰，在其鈕扣上掛上個金香包，誰便成了皇后。

民間對香包的使用更為普遍，除男女老幼可佩飾掛戴外，也作禮品贈送。《紅樓夢》裏就有許多次描述。一些青年男女更是珍重，常把香包作為私定終身的表記，豫劇《香囊記》中一對失散多年的夫妻就是靠一隻香包，才得團圓的。當然，隨着社會的發展，科學的進步，這些作用已蕩然無存了，但香包依然受到人們的喜愛。它的造型極為豐富，小巧玲瓏，芳香宜人，不僅是傳統的可觀賞的工藝品，還有一定的防病保健作用。在民間也是青年男女寄托情思的禮品。它多以瓜果蔬菜、花鳥蟲魚、小動物、琴棋書卷、日用器物及風情人物為對象，表達了人們不同的審美情趣。

鳳翔縣八十歲老人王銀鳳的金絲香包，匠心獨運，別具一格，做工精巧，受到中外朋友的稱讚。在千陽一帶結婚時，新房的門簾上沿也有掛香包的習俗。

Many traditional and folk customs are related to the Duanwu Festival, or the Dragon Boat Festival which falls on the 5th day of the 5th lunar month. One of them is making the perfume pouch (commonly called xiangbao, xiangnang, xiangdai or hebao). The custom has been practiced from early times. It is said that people in ancient times used to carry a medicine bag when went hunting to drive out poisonous insects. Today we still find some old men carry on them a bag in the shape of calabash, a custom that can probably be traced to the old tradition.

Another old saying goes that when Qu Yuan, a great poet of the Chu state in the Warring States Period, drowned himself in Miluo River on the 5th day of the 5th lunar month, people in the neighbouring Qin, out of sympathy for and to cherish the memory of him, made and carried on them the xiangbao stuffed with the sweetgrass and perfumes that he had loved. Some people say it is a long-standing custom of the Han people; its origin can be traced to the Tang dynasty when women in the rural areas would in the 4th lunar month each year begin to make xiangbao with coloured silk, silk threads and gold and silver beads. By the Qing dynasty, xiangbao was carried by people not only on the Dragon Boat Festival, but every day, because the Manchus had long had the custom. According to the Qing custom, emperors and empresses were required to carry xiangbao on them all the year round and at the end of every year, or on important festivals, the emperor would award the princes and ministers each a xiangbao to show his favour for them. More interestingly perfume pouches were used by Emperor Tongzhi and Emperor Guanxu in choosing their empresses: The girls were line up to be examined by the emperor, who would hang a perfume pouch on the button on the dress of the girl whom he took a fancy to.

The common people make an even more extensive use of the perfume pouch. They —— men and women, old and young —— all can carry one on them and can present it to others as a gift. There are many descriptions of such practice in the Chinese classical novel *Dream of the Red*

*Mansion.* Some young men and women often use it as a token of love. There is a Yu opera, *Story of a Perfume Pouch*, which tells the story that a married couple who have been separated and have had no news of each other for years finally come together and are reunited —— with the help of a perfume pouch. Of course, with the development of human society and the advance of science, the perfume pouch has long lost such functions. But it remains in the favour of many. It takes a wide variety of shapes, but whatever shape it is always small and exquisite and has a pleasing fragrance. It is not only a delicate work of art, but it also has some preventive power against diseases. Among the young country folks, it is still a valued gift to be exchanged between lovers. Decorations range from floral and small animal (such as bird and fish) designs to patterns of musical instruments, books, utensils and romantic figures, depending on the maker's aesthetic taste.

The perfume pouch made of gold filaments by the 80-year-old Wang Yinfeng of Fengxiang county is an artifact of fine workmanship and is unique in its style. It has been praised by many foreign friends. In Qianyang area, an old custom has still been kept up that the door curtain of the bridal chamber is adorned with perfume pouches.

虎香包（鳳翔）
Perfume pouch embroidered with a tiger (Fengxiang)

香包（西安）
Perfume pouches (Xi'an)

蟈蚱香包（澄城）
Perfume pouch embroidered with
grasshoppers (Chengcheng)

燈籠香包
Perfume pouch embroidered
with lanterns

金魚、蠶香包（渭南）
Perfume pouches embroidered with
goldfish or silkworms (Weinan)

蟈蚱、兔、花香包（澄城）
Perfume pouches embroidered with grasshoppers, rabbits and flowers (Chengcheng)

魚香包（鳳翔）
Perfume pouch embroidered with fish (Fengxiang)

獅子香包（鳳翔王銀鳳）
Perfume pouch embroidered with a lion (made by Wang Yinfeng of Fengxiang)

# 草 編
## STRAW ARTICLES

草編在中國有較久遠的歷史，遠在五、六千年前，編織的技術就已出現（在半坡和臨潼姜寨等原始遺址出土的陶器底部就印有清晰的蓆紋痕迹），先民們就用野生的葛、麻等以斜紋、棋盤紋等結構形式做成編織物。幾千年來，發展、演變，勞動人民充分利用當地所產原材料，不斷創造革新，形成有獨特風格民間工藝品。

在關中以玉米棒殼、麥稈爲主，經過精心設計，編成各種實用而美觀的生活日用品，在材料質地美的基礎上，給予多種美的變化，強調其形式美感。有提籃、座墊、草帽、果盒、地墊、壁掛、盆墊等多種樣式。有的還利用事先染有各色的草料加以裝飾，大部分是用原料本色（經漂白）組合形成多樣的圖案紋飾。一些大型地墊、草蓆，根據設計圖樣，在有經緯綫的本框架上，按要求格式有順序的編織，紋樣不斷出新，豐富多采。在關中以武功、興平、鳳翔、渭南等產地爲主，一般農家在麥收、秋收時就已在採集上等用料，一有閑時，人人動手編草，甚至七、八歲小姑娘都會編草編。這是草編工藝的第一道工序，富有農村生活樂趣，編得快而細的爲優等，待積聚相當數量後，再集中加工製作。

陝南有藤編、竹編、棕編、麻編，陝北有柳編、高粱稈編等，品種繁多，形式多樣。

草編經濟實用，造型新巧，在現代生活中，顯示了它特有的鄉土藝術魅力。

Straw Articles are of great antiquity in China. As early as 5,000–6,000 years ago, our remote ancestors already knew how to weave, plait or braid kudzu vine, hemp or other natural fibers into some simple articles of diagonal or checkerboard patterns. (Some pottery objects excavated from the primitive ruins at Banpo and Jiangzhai in Lintong show clear imprints of straw mats on their bottoms.) Since then, the labouring people, through successive generations, have made constant innovations and gradually turned this human endeavour into a distinctive sort of folk art.

Guanzhong in middle Shaanxi mainly produces articles made of cornhusk and wheat straw. They are articles for daily use, such as baskets, cushions, hats, fruit boxies, doormats, pot mats and wall hangings. They all are elegantly designed and, based on the natural beauty of the materials, seek to have variations in represention, with emphasis on the beauty of shape. Most of them exploit the natural colour of the materal (after bleached) to form a variety of patterns, and some are decoratively coloured. Some large mats and mattresses, woven in accordance with special designs, can show many patterns. Wugong, Xinping, Fengxiang and Weinan are the main producing areas of these straw articles in Guanzhong. The peasants usually begin collecting first-grade materials at the wheat and maize harvests and do the weaving work in slack seasons. Even girls of 7 or 8 years old could do straw weaving. They all take delight in the work —— it is a joy of country life.

In the south of the privince there are rattan work, and articles made of bamboo, palm fiber and hemp, and in the north, wickerwork and articles made of sorghum stalk.

Because they are inexpensive, useful and beautiful, and, more importantly, because they have the rural artistic charm, straw articles have won themselves an admirable place in modern life.

麥草編: 草帽 (鳳翔)
Straw hat (Fengxiang)

玉米棒殼: 坐墊 (武功)
Cornhusk mats (Wugong)

玉米棒殼: 門墊（武功）
Door mat made of cornhusk
(Wugong)

麥草與籐編: 籃（鳳翔）
Straw and rattan baskets
(Fengxiang)

麥草編: 提籃（鳳翔）
Straw baskets (Fengxiang)

麥草編: 古代車馬人提籃（鳳翔）
Straw baskets decorated with
ancient carriages, horses and
figures (Fengxiang)

麥草編: 孔雀開屏提籃（鳳翔）
Straw basket decorated with a
peacock in his pride (Fengxiang)

# 花 饃
## DECORATED STEAMED-BUN

逢年過節，老人過壽，小孩滿月、過歲，婚喪嫁娶或獻奠祖先，在農村有製作花饃（也叫面花）作爲贈送禮品和祭祀供品的古老鄉俗。

作面花，也是"比巧巧"形式之一，表現了淳樸善良的農家婦女們的心靈手巧和藝術想像力。每年清明節時，來到炎黃子孫的敬祖聖地——軒轅皇帝陵，憑吊這位中華民族的始祖時，我們便可欣賞到各地羣衆精心製作的千姿百態的面花藝術，做得講究、豐富，寄托了黃帝的後裔的悠悠古情。

面花，是以上等小麥粉爲主料，用剪刀、木梳、頂針、細竹筒、燈芯等，通過巧手捏塑成各種花飾，以武火猛蒸而成，待新出籠的花饃熱氣未消時，用食品色點染，花花綠綠，各顯異態，情趣盎然。

花饃的花飾以神態自然的花鳥蟲魚蝴蝶、蔬菜雜果、猴獻桃等萬物生靈爲主，表達對祖先的祭祀、老輩的祝福、新婚夫婦的恭賀和對美好生活的熱愛、嚮往。五月端午或嬰孩滿月時，由舅家送給外甥一個特製的大型圓圈面花，羣衆叫"曲蓮"，上面捏塑着魚、龍、蓮花之類，魚指五穀豐登，吉慶有餘；龍指時運亨通，青雲直上；蓮指幸福花開，喜氣盈門。

花饃的內容共同象徵着吉祥如意，寄寓着人們深厚而美好的感情。它反映與表現着特定的民族心理與性格。

On New Year and some other festivals, on the birthday of an elder man/woman, or when an infant is a month old, or attending a wedding or funeral, or holding a ceremony for ancestors —— on all these occasions people in rural areas would make special steamed buns which are coloured and decorated with stylized plant, floral or figural designs, to be given out as gifts or as offerings. This custom has been practised from early times.

This special kind of steamed buns are commonly called *huamo* (literally, "flowered bun") or *mianhua* (literally, "dough flower"). Country women customarily look upon the making of *mianhua* as an informal contest of their cleverness, deftness and artistic imagination. On the Qing Ming Festival each year, when people come from all places to visit the Mausoleum of Emperor Xuan Yuan, the legendary earliest ancestor of the Chinese nation, one can see there all sorts of the finely made *mianhua* the pilgrims bring there as offerings.

*Mianhua* is made of dough, the primary ingredient of which is fine wheat flour. The process of its making is roughly like this: With the help of such tools as scissors, comb, thimble, thin bamboo tube and straw, the dough is kneaded and molded into various patterns, then steamed in high heat, and finally dip-dyed in eatable colours.

The more popular decoration designs are flowers, birds, insects, fish, butterflies, vegetables, fruits, or "the monkey presents you with peaches." They represent memory and worship of ancestors, blessings for elders, congratulations to the newly married, or just aspirations for a better life.

On the Dragon Boat Festival or when a baby is a month old, the brother of the infant's mother will sent it a specially made, large *mianhua* ring (called "winding lotus), decorated with fish, dragon and lotus designs. The fish represents bumper harvests; the dragon, good luck; and the lotus, happiness.

In general, all the motifs symbolize good luck and embody the people's deep love for the beautiful. They are reflections of the psychology and characted of a nation under given circumstances.

洛川花饃
Steamed Buns from
Luochuan county

洛川花馍
Steamed Buns from
Luochuan county

洛川花馍
Steamed Buns from
Luochuan county

澄城花饃
Steamed Buns from
Chengcheng county

澄城花饃
Steamed Buns from
Chengcheng county

澄城花饃
Steamed Buns from
Chengcheng county

澄城花饃
Steamed Buns from
Chengcheng county

# 農民畫
# PEASANT PAINTING

我國的當代民間繪畫藝術——農民畫，近些年來，以它獨特的民間藝術手法反映現實生活而躋身於世界藝術之林，受到中外朋友讚譽。

陝西起步較早的戶縣農民畫已有近三十年的發展史，成爲全國知名的“農民畫鄉”，在國內外多次展出中受到好評。現在，又有安塞、洛川、宜君、眉縣等地新的作者隊伍如雨後春筍，創作了不少有地方藝術特色和濃郁生活氣息的作品。

面對這些質樸的勞動者的畫，廣袤大地的泥土芳香，莊戶人家的音容笑貌，社會主義農村的盎然生氣迎面撲來。這些田園風貌、風情民俗的形象寫照，流露出勞動者袒直而眞誠，憨厚而風趣的性格，有種撩動心緒的藝術魅力。

農民畫大致可以說是由傳統的民間剪紙、刺繡、壁畫發展而來。從宜君農民畫中可察覺到較多地保留了傳統藝術大膽誇張、大幅度變形和凝練明快的藝術特色。農民畫善於從平凡的鄉村生活中挖掘新意，既有時代感，又融進獨特的鄉土風情，傾向於單純和自由的表現，直抒胸臆，感情熱烈奔放，帶有一定的浪漫色彩，已走向藝術創作的自由天地。

Peasant painting, as a comtemporary form of Chinese folk painting, has in recent years made a niche in the temple of the arts of the world. It has won international praise for its unique artistic style in representing life.

Peasant painting in Huxian County, Shaanxi Province, has claimed a history for development, and the county has become China's well-known "land of peasant painting." The many works of the county's peasant artists received much public praise during exhibitions at home and abroad. Now peasant artists are also emerging in large numbers in Ansai, Luochuan, Yijun and Meixian counties and have created a number of works with local characteristics and a rich flavour of life.

Standing before these unsophisticated paintings, you can feel they are diffusing the aroma of the earth, see in them the vivid images of the country people, and experience the vigour of socialist countryside. They are portrayals of rural scene and life, and illustrations of folk custom. Reflecting the labourers' straightforwardness and honesty and their cheerful and humorous disposition, they have the artistic charm that evoke aesthetic emotion.

Generally speaking, peasant painting has evolved from traditional paper-cutting, embroidery and mural painting. Traces of such traditional artistic techniques as exaggeration and distortion, as well as the traditionally concise and bright artistic style, are highly discernible in the Yijun peasant paintings. Good at discovering new aspects of the seemingly familiar country life, peasant painting has some of the characteristics of modern arts, while at the same time it incorporates in itself the singular rural style. It tends to make simple and free representations of life, expressing straightforwardly what the artist thinks or feels. It is usually overflowing with strong emotion, and is somewhat romantic. With respect to artistic creation, it has begun moving toward the realm of freedom.

傳經（戶縣劉豐濤）
Passing on experience (Liu
Fengtao, Huxian)

集路行歌（戶縣李周成）
Singing all the way to the market
place (Li Zhoucheng, Huxian)

春到奶鄉（戶縣樊志華）
Spring on a dairy farm (Fan
Zhihua, Huxian)

娶親（戶縣劉金花）
Wedding ceremony (Liu Jinhua, Huxian)

花鼓（洛川王中學）
Flower-drum (Wang Zhongxue, Luochuan)

看戲（戶縣王景龍）
Seeing an opera (Wang Jinglong,
Huxian)

賣泥人（戶縣雒志儉）
Selling clay figurines (Luo Zhijian,
Huxian)

# 社火面譜與社火
# SHEHUO TYPES OF FACIAL MAKE-UP

　　臉譜是傳統戲曲中演員面部化妝的一種程式，主要用於淨角。這種藝術可追溯到古代的儺舞和唐朝的代面，而且保留了不少遠古的神話人物形象。大量表現神靈精怪及歷史傳說人物的臉譜圖案，奇瑰傳神，變化多端，效果強烈。各種人物大都有特定的譜式和色彩，達到"人可以相貌"、"知人知面就知心"的藝術效果。

　　社火臉譜的構圖、勾畫、塗色，注重眉、眼、嘴的裝飾。它從人物的性格和容貌特徵出發，以誇張的手法描畫五官的部位和膚色，進而突出面部的骨骼、筋絡、肌肉紋理，全在於突出表現各類人物善惡的內在本質，強調色彩對比，古樸而豪放，有着強烈的象徵性。它與戲曲服裝、盔頭的色彩裝飾相輔相成，相互輝映，從而形成了完整的、直觀的具有民族特色的戲曲人物造型。

　　這裏介紹的是用木雕敷彩和紙殼製成的可掛起來欣賞的藝術品。

　　社火，是節日扮演的各種雜戲，熱鬧非凡的民間娛樂活動。起源很早，可追溯到隋唐年間，過去亦稱"射虎"，在取其以正壓邪和祈求萬事如意、五穀豐登、人畜平安之意。南宋詩人范成大曾說過："民間鼓樂謂之"社火"，不可悉記，大抵以滑稽取笑"。又傳是古代祭祀活動中的一種表演。現在已成為較普遍的迎春喜慶活動。

　　它是一種綜合藝術，既講究化妝的造型美、鑼鼓的音樂美、程式的舞蹈美，又着力於境界的意趣美，令人可看、可聽、可思，獲得美感。

　　在農曆正月十五前後，這種活動達到高潮，城鎮鄉里選出精明強壯的青年男女、兒童，裝扮成各種戲曲人物，組成一齣一齣雜戲，連成隊伍，游行表演，這時鑼鼓齊鳴，鞭炮震天，男女老少爭相觀看。社火因地域、鄉俗的不同而各具特色。它的內容和形式名目繁多。表演技巧，一般講究壯麗、驚險、滑稽、俏美、灑脫。在整個社火活動中，民間美術廣泛地顯示了它裝飾性、鄉土味很濃的審美情趣。

"Types of facial make-up," as its is used here and elsewhere in this book, is a special terminology referring to those types of facial make-up worn by characters, particularly the "painted face" type of characters, in traditional Chinese operas. This art of make-up probably owes its origin to the exorcistical dances of ancient times and the "daimian" (a dance drama) of the Tang dynasty. The types of facial-make-up today still retain many features of the images of the mythological figures in remote antiquity. A considerable number of such facial make-up patterns representing gods, demons or legendary figures look quaint, vivid, colourful, and highly impressive. Different types of characters have different types of facail make-up in their distinctive colours, with the result —— or the artistic effect —— that their personality can be readily recognized by the type of make-up they wear.

Shehuo refers to a variety of operas performed on some local festivals. The types of facial make-up in these operas, in respect to their composition, delineation and painting, lay stress on the ornamentation of eyebrows, eyes and mouth. In accordance with the temperament or personality of a character, as well as his facial features, the five sense organs —— ears, eyes, lips, nose and tongue —— are exaggeratedly delineated and painted to give prominence to facial bones, sinews and muscles. The purpose is to clearly illustrate the good or evil nature of the character. Colours are used in such a way as to bring out glaring contrast between them. The characters's antique, fantastic and highly symbolic make-up matches well with their fanciful costumes and richly ornamented helmets, and together they make a complete, characteristic representation of the persons of a drama.

The illustrations given here are reproductions of the painted faces carved out of wood or made of cardboard which, as works of art, can be hung up for a show.

Shehuo dates back to the Sui and Tang dynasties, when it was called "Shehu" ("shooting tiger") with the intentions of the righteous overwhelming the wicked, and the wishes for good luck, rich harvest of all crops and safety of both men and livestocks. Fan Chengda, a poet of the Southern Song synasty, said: "The folk music accompanied by drumbeats is called Shehuo. It is difficult to elaborate it, but, for the most part, it is comic." Another view attributes its origin to a performance during memorial ceremonies for gods or ancestors in anciet times. But now it has become part of the festivities on the advent of spring.

Shehuo is a comprehensive art of facial make-up, music (discoursed by a band of gongs and drums), and dancing (with stylized movements): it is a sort of audio-visual art that can afford an aesthetic satisfaction to the audience.

The Shehuo festivities reach their climax around the 15th of the first lunar month, when the villages and rural towns would select the cleverest and strongest from among their youngmen and young women as well as children to play the various parts in the operas. They act in a parading procession to the accompaniment of gongs and drums and crackers, attracting a large audience.

In both content and form, Shehuo varies from place to place because of their different local customs, but in general they all pay great attention to giving a magnificent, breathtaking, comic, graceful and free-wheeling performance. In all the Shehuo activities, folks arts fully demonstrate their decorative effect and strong rural aesthetic taste.

社火芯子（西安）
Shehuo wicks (Xi'an)

軒轅皇帝（寶鷄）
Emperor Xuan Yuan (Baoji)

邳彤／漢光武大將
Pi Tong, Emperor Guang Wu's
general, Han dynasty

馬武／漢光武大將
Ma Wu, Emperor Guang Wu's
general, Han dynasty

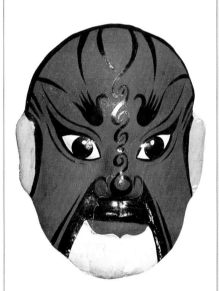

關羽（寶鷄）
Guan Yu (Baoji)

張飛／《三國演義》中人物
Zhang Fei, a character in the novel
*The Romance of the Three
Kingdoms*

巨靈神／神話戲《大鬧天宮》中的人物
Ju Lingshen (God Ju Ling), a
character in the opera *Revolt
Against Heavan*

楊戩（二郎神）╱《封神演義》人物
The God Erlang, a character in
*Canonization of the Gods*

雷震子╱《封神演義》中人物
Lei Zhenzi, a character in
*Canonization of the Gods*

廣成子╱《封神演義》中人物
Guang Chengzi, a character in the
mythological novel *Canonization of
the Gods*

野苗╱社火戲中《神農氏拿野苗》人物
Ye Miao, a character in the Shehuo
opera *Shennong Captures Ye Miao*

單于王╱《蘇武牧羊》中的匈奴王
King Chanyu, chief of the Xiongnu
in the opera *Su Wu Tends Sheep*

鼠怪╱《老君收七怪》中一怪
Rat Demon, one of the demons
described in *Lao Jun Subdues
Seven Demons*

古城燈市（西安）
Lantern market in the ancient city
(Xi'an)

耍龍燈
Dragon lantern

獅舞（西安）
Lion dance (Xi'an)

牛鬥虎（周至）
Ox and tiger locked in a fight
(Zhouzhi)

猪八戒背媳婦（西安）
Zhu Bajie carries his wife on his
back (Xi'an)

高蹺（西安）
Stilts (Xi'an)

抬神爐（韓城）
Carrying the Holy Furance
(Hancheng)

韓城百面鑼鼓
Gongs and drums of Hancheng

老秧歌（洛川）
Old Yangge dance (Luochuan)

跑馬（洛川）
Riding a horse (Luochuan)

蹾鼓（洛川）
Bie Drum dance (Luochuan)

# 陝西民間美術分佈簡況圖

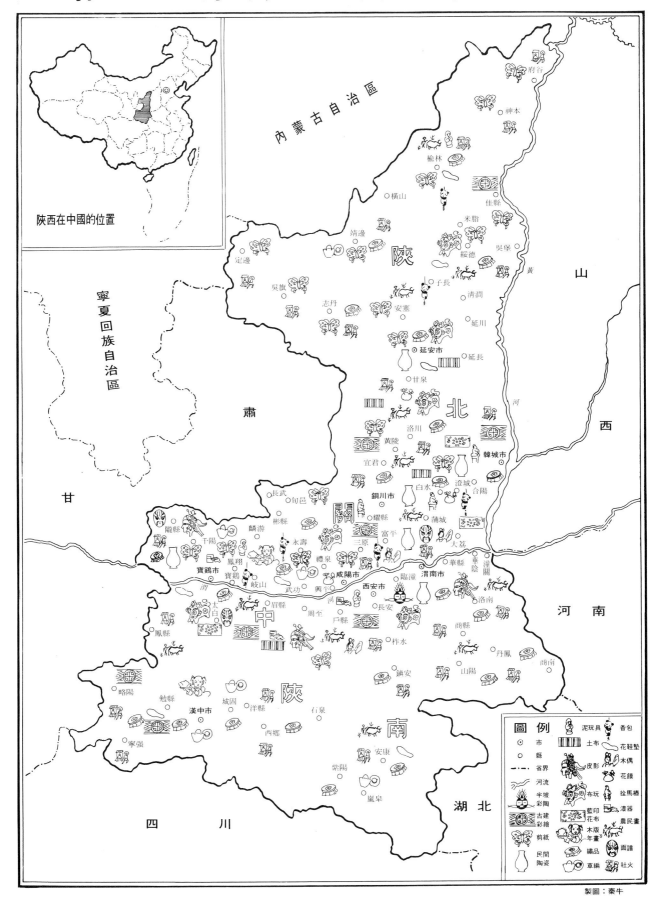

陝西在中國的位置

內蒙古自治區

寧夏回族自治區

甘　肅

陝　北

山　西

河　南

關　中

陝　南

四　川

湖　北

府谷
神木
榆林
橫山
佳縣
米脂
靖邊
綏德
吳堡
定邊
吳旗
志丹
安塞
子長
清澗
延川
延安市
延長
甘泉
洛川
黃陵
韓城市
宜君
白水
澄城
合陽
銅川市
耀縣
蒲城
長武
旬邑
彬縣
麟游
永壽
富平
三原
大荔
隴縣
千陽
鳳翔
岐山
寶雞市
寶雞
武功
興平
咸陽
禮泉
西安市
周至
戶縣
長安
渭南市
臨潼
華縣
華陰
潼關
洛南
太白
眉縣
商縣
柞水
鳳縣
略陽
勉縣
城固
洋縣
漢中市
西鄉
石泉
鎮安
山陽
丹鳳
商南
寧強
安康
紫陽
嵐皋

## 圖　例

- 市
- 縣
- 省界
- 河流
- 半坡彩陶
- 古建彩繪
- 剪紙
- 民間陶瓷
- 泥玩具
- 土布
- 皮影
- 布玩
- 藍印花布
- 木版年畫
- 繡品
- 草編
- 香包
- 花鞋墊
- 木偶
- 花饃
- 拴馬樁
- 漆器
- 農民畫
- 面譜
- 社火

製圖：秦牛